Business Thought Leaders from India

Business Thought Leaders from India

The Best Ideas on Innovation, Management, Strategy, and Leadership

STUART CRAINER + DES DEARLOVE

New York   Chicago   San Francisco   Athens   London   Madrid
Mexico City   Milan   New Delhi   Singapore   Sydney   Toronto

1 2 3 4 5 6 7 8 9 0   DOC/DOC   1 2 0 9 8 7 6 5 4

ISBN   978-0-07-182756-0
MHID   0-07-182756-0

e-ISBN   978-0-07-182753-9
e-MHID   0-07-182753-6

Library of Congress Cataloging-in-Publication Data
Crainer, Stuart.
  Thinkers 50 business thought leaders from India : the best ideas on innovation,
management, strategy, and leadership / by Stuart Crainer and Des Dearlove.
     pages cm
  ISBN 978-0-07-182756-0 (paperback) — ISBN 0-07-182756-0 (paperback)
  1. Management—India. 2. Strategic planning—India. 3. Leadership—India.
4. Executives—India—Case studies. I. Dearlove, Des. II. Title.
  HD70.I4C73 2014
  658.4—dc23
                                                        2014011602

McGraw-Hill Education books are available at special quantity discounts to
use as premiums and sales promotions or for use in corporate training
programs. To contact a representative, please visit the Contact Us pages at
www.mhprofessional.com.

Contents

Introduction   vii

CHAPTER 1   The Rise of Indian Thinking   1

CHAPTER 2   The Ghoshal Legacy   15

CHAPTER 3   Pyramid Thinking: C. K. Prahalad   27

CHAPTER 4   Making It Happen: Ram Charan and Subir Chowdhury   49

CHAPTER 5   Innovation Indian Style: From VG to Jugaad   73

CHAPTER 6   Global Voices: Pankaj Ghemawat and Anil K. Gupta   97

CHAPTER 7   India Inc.   117

CHAPTER 8   The Kings of Context   133

CHAPTER 9   Thinking at Work   157

              Acknowledgments   167

              Index   169

Introduction

This is indeed India; the land of dreams and romance,
of fabulous wealth and fabulous poverty, of splendor
and rags, of palaces and hovels, of famine and pesti-
lence, of genii and giants and Aladdin lamps, of tigers
and elephants, the cobra and the jungle, the country
of a thousand nations and a hundred tongues, of a
thousand religions and two million gods, cradle of the
human race, birthplace of human speech, mother of
history, grandmother of legend, great-grandmother of
tradition. . . .

Mark Twain, *Following the Equator*, 1897

India is an enigma wrapped in ancient mysteries, a fast-growing
modern economic powerhouse with perennial and deep-rooted
problems, a success story laced with tragedy.

The first impression of India is its sheer scale. A union of 28 states and seven union territories, India is the second most populous country in the world, with 1,210,193,422 people recorded in the 2011 national census. A single state, Uttar Pradesh, has more people than Brazil, the sixth most populous country in the world.

And then there is color and confusion.

Over recent years, as we have charted the economic rise of this great nation and the challenges it still faces, we have been fortunate enough to meet some of the nation's finest business thinkers. They have informed and changed our views on India and on business and life more generally.

India invigorates, and the same thing can be said of the thinkers whose work we have highlighted at the Thinkers50.

Des Dearlove and Stuart Crainer
Thinkers50 Founders

Business Thought Leaders from India

The Rise of Indian Thinking

The rarefied world of business thinking has been largely American terrain over the last hundred years. From Frederick Taylor with his stopwatch at the beginning of the twentieth century to the modern generation of gurus, Americans have monopolized business wisdom. Even the brief love affair with Japanese business practices in the early 1980s was intellectually colonized by American thinkers such as W. Edwards Deming and Richard Pascale.

Now change is in the air. A new generation of thinkers and ideas is emerging from India and elsewhere. Superstars in the business guru firmament over recent years have included C. K. Prahalad, coauthor of the bestselling *Competing for the Future*; the itinerant executive coach Ram Charan; the Nobel laureate in economics Amartya Sen; Vijay Govindarajan, professor of international business at Dartmouth College's Tuck School of Business; and London Business School's Sumantra Ghoshal.

There are many others. Indian business thinking has entered the mainstream.

"The thinkers are often first-generation immigrants to the West. Almost all have had firsthand experience working in typically chaotic Indian businesses," says Dr. Gita Piramal, founder of the Indian management magazine *The Smart Manager*. "Some, like Sumantra, worked in the public sector. C.K.'s first job was in Union Carbide's battery factory in Chennai, and he also worked in a company making pistons. Ram Charan was born and brought up as part of an extended family of 13 that ran a shoe shop. All pulled themselves out of India, and many have a Harvard link."* Indeed, the current dean of Harvard Business School is the Indian-born Nitin Nohria.

More will undoubtedly follow. The world's MBA programs have a growing number of Indian students. This is not just an American phenomenon. When last we checked, the biggest national contingent at France's business school INSEAD was Indian. The same is true of many other business schools throughout the world.

"God does not discriminate across countries on intelligence. So if you say that 20 percent of people are smart, that means 200 million smart Indians, and that's a lot of human capital," notes Tuck's Vijay Govindarajan. "At the same time, there is no doubt that Indians have had a disproportionate influence on management thinking and practice. As a percentage of the U.S. popula-

---

* All quotes are from our interviews unless otherwise stated.

tion they are minuscule—less than a single percent—but look at their representation in business schools. I remember when I got my job at Tuck 20 years ago I was the first Indian faculty member. Now it's not unusual to see 20 percent of the faculty with Indian roots and connections."

Rising to the Top

Vijay Govindarajan explains the reasons Indian thinkers have risen to positions of influence: "Like other first-generation immigrants we had a tremendous hunger to succeed. For us, there was no safety net. But there are other elements to this. Indians have a strong work ethic, speak English, and have been traditionally influenced by American education and educational institutions. Indians are good at conceptual thinking and analysis. Another very important quality is that we tend to be very patient—a great virtue in teaching." Govindarajan originally trained as a chartered accountant in India, won a Ford Foundation scholarship to Harvard, and is now one of the highest-earning executive speakers and a prolific author.

Another perspective comes from Professor Nirmalya Kumar of London Business School, now director of strategy at Tata. "Business is well respected in India as it was the only way to make a decent living besides being a doctor until India reformed in 1990. Thus, the talent pool that went into business PhDs in the United States from India was excellent. It became a preferred option to escape India after finishing at the country's top technology schools. Some of these PhDs then became the gurus of today."

Personal ambition is a powerful driver, but what it doesn't explain is why Indian thinkers have become so influential with

Western business audiences. Position and influence are often not synonymous. It is one thing to become a Harvard professor, quite another to have the ear of Fortune 100 CEOs. Ram Charan, for example, was a confidant to Jack Welch when Welch was running GE and was coauthor with Larry Bossidy of *Execution: The Discipline of Getting Things Done.* C. K. Prahalad topped the Thinkers50 in 2007 and 2009. This story made the front page of *The Times of India.* Sumantra Ghoshal, with coauthor Chris Bartlett of Harvard, wrote *Managing Across Borders: The Transnational Solution*, which was named by the *Financial Times* as one of the 50 most influential business books of the century. The list goes on.

What does this hill of ideas amount to?

An Indian School of Management?

One obvious conclusion is that it signifies the development of a distinctively Indian school of management, but this tends to be played down by Indian thinkers. There appears to be no definitive Indian way.

However, the increasing influence of Indian thinkers coincides with a period of introspection into the nature and purpose of Western capitalism. After Enron and the 2008 financial meltdown, there has been disillusionment with the individualistic model, a sense that corporate America has been a breeding ground for executives whose personal greed and egos eclipsed their sense of public duty. Indian thinking taps into this debate. India's collectivist culture offers a foil to America's rampant individualism. Among Indian thinkers there is a keen sense of capitalism's ethical and societal obligations—witness C. K. Prahalad's most groundbreaking book, *The Fortune at the Bottom of the Pyramid*, which advocated a new approach to business to take account of micro-markets among the world's poor.

The Future of Competition, the book Prahalad coauthored in 2004, also examined how the balance of power is changing between the rich and the poor. The book's core idea is to move the debate from a firm- and product-centered view of value that has persisted for over 75 years to a view of value based on the co-creation of unique personalized experiences.

The importance of the sense of responsibility in the Indian take on capitalism was brought home to us when we talked to Ravi Kant, then chairman of Tata Motors. The Tata Group was formed in 1868 by Jamsetji Nusserwanji Tata, who with his sons created two public charitable trusts and gave their entire share-holdings to those trusts. Today the trusts control nearly two-thirds of Tata Sons, the holding company that oversees more than 100 Tata companies operating in over 80 countries.

"Each company is governed by its own independent board of directors and has its own strategy and listings; however, each company is connected with the group by adhering to certain values and processes. Ratan Tata, the group chairman, and his family own a very small percentage of shares, so there is a strong concept of trusteeship, not ownership, throughout all the companies. Mr. Tata heads the Tata Group by virtue of being trustee of those trusts and not as the owner, and that perspective permeates throughout the management levels within the company," Ravi Kant explained. "This is one dimension to how we manage. The second is that the founder, when he started setting up businesses, had the very devolutionary idea that whatever comes from society should go back to the society in some form or other. That means you hold in trust what you are getting from the society, and you give it back to the society.

"Thus, Tata has a very different kind of culture or ethos, and this permeates the entire Tata Group, which leads to better corporate governance. Under this approach, there are better ethical values, different ways of doing things, and better records of showing concern for society. There is a greater caring for people and caring for things around our businesses. Tata's values and group culture are unique."

Synthesizing

The ability to reconcile conflicting views and experiences is an integral part of the Indian culture. This informs the way Indians manage and lead.

"Many Indians growing up in the United States detect an inconsistency or incoherence about modern life, which for Indian-born people like my parents is very, very difficult," says Harvard Business School's Rakesh Khurana. "Somehow you are supposed to be moral and generous in your private life, but that doesn't apply when you go to work—you don't have to be the same person. That kind of role fragmentation or inconsistency was really seen as profane. One must find a way that synthesizes both who you are in private and who you are in public life and work. One has to find a role that creates integrity. In India they are also dealing with the issue of how do you reconcile traditionalism, where there's a lot of meaning and symbolism imbued in everyday life and family and community, with making sure you get the benefits and individual spark of modern society."

Khurana points to the fusion seen in Indian Bhangra music—a synthesis of modern dance and traditional music—and the questions raised in literature by Indian authors such as the Nobel laureate V. S. Naipaul and Arundhati Roy. "People are trying to find a synthesis between the benefits of modernity without losing the meaning associated with traditional structures such as family. A growing number of people are uncomfortable with the winner-take-all markets as they currently exist and that the indicator of one's worth in the world is perfectly correlated to the size of their bank accounts. Another key question for them is how we can enjoy the advantages of modernity—but without a 50 percent divorce rate."

Raising such questions lies at the heart of much of Indian business thinking and practice. It is not that Indian thinkers are negative about the Western business world. Indeed, they tend to be enthusiastic in their praise of the opportunities on offer. But they offer a unique viewpoint, the best of both worlds.

Two-Way Learning

Increasing Indian economic prosperity has posed new questions for accepted Western business best practices. The abundance of fresh material from India is challenging and reshaping existing thinking. Business thinkers with Indian experience and sensibilities are well placed to make sense of this.

It is clear that the flow of knowledge has changed. Indian businesspeople traditionally learned from American business schools. The flow of knowledge is now two-way. The assumption in the past was that other emerging markets could learn from

India. Now it is recognized that Western companies and executives can also learn from India.

The leading Indian thinkers remain in close contact with their home country. The late Sumantra Ghoshal, for example, was the founding dean of the Indian School of Business in Hyderabad. C. K. Prahalad also remained acutely aware of his Indian roots. Prahalad drew attention to the world's 4 billion poorest consumers who are aspiring to a better life and demanding more goods and services. "This situation represents a huge opportunity for companies to change their mindsets and their business models (e.g., 'the poor can't afford or have no use for consumer products' or 'we can't make money in this market')," he said. "The real source of market promise is not the wealthy few in the developing world or even the emerging middle-income consumers. It is the billions of aspiring poor who are joining the market economy for the first time."

Indian thinking challenges existing business practice and received wisdom. "Many American companies say they have globalized, but they are really international rather than global. They are beginning to realize that the center of gravity cannot simply be the United States. They have traditionally developed products for the U.S. market and then tried to export them to other markets. That is increasingly obsolete. To conquer markets like India requires sophisticated thinking," says Vijay Govindarajan.

A Passage to India

The new generation of Indian thinkers offers a challenge to the conventional view of globalization. Globalization was previously seen as the triad of United States–Europe–Asia (meaning mainly

Japan). India was usually overlooked as a hapless economic pygmy, filed under emerging—slowly. Now Indian thinkers—people such as Pankaj Ghemawat—are helping executives see globalization in its totality.

"There's a much greater sensitivity and sense that the centers of the economic future may be more than simply the traditional Western European and North American nexus," observes Rakesh Khurana.

Adds Vijay Govindarajan: "The United States and Europe are congested and highly contested markets. In China and India there is still virgin territory. As markets and sources of ideas and innovation they need to be taken seriously."

The fact that the radar screen now extends beyond America's borders is itself an important development. Perhaps the true appeal of the Indian gurus is that they do not automatically regard the United States as the center of the commercial universe. They offer a different lens through which to look at issues such as globalization and shareholder value and even the purpose of business. In doing so they pose questions about which Americans are sometimes blind.

As the late Sumantra Ghoshal observed: "A very different management philosophy is arising and will become dominant—the purpose, process, people philosophy. We are moving beyond strategy to purpose, beyond structure to process, and beyond systems to people. This will shift the basic doctrine of shareholder capitalism and moderate it so that if people are adding the most value, then people will increasingly have to be seen as investors, not as employees. Shareholders invest money and expect a return on their money and expect capital growth. People will be seen in the same way. So they will invest their human capital in the company, will expect a return on it, and expect growth of that capital."

Ghoshal's legacy lives on. He mentored and then extensively coauthored with Nitin Nohria and inspired his students toward a more holistic view of management and leadership and the way it is linked to the broader society. "Nitin and I have been coauthoring papers and cases on management as a profession," says Rakesh Khurana. "A profession not simply in a technical sense but in a normative sense that considers things like responsibility, mutual respect for the various constituents in a business enterprise such as employees and customers, and accountability. Ideas that were catalyzed through discussions with Sumantra."

Coping with Ambiguity

The Indian managers we have encountered and worked with appear ideally equipped to meet the challenges of our times. To them, uncertainty is a fact of life.

This was something we posed to Kiron Ravindran, a professor at Spain's IE Business School:

> I grew up in the Middle East, I've lived in India, studied and lived in the United States for eight years. I've been in Europe now for four years. I see different people, and one of the things that have helped me is that I can deal with different kinds of people from different backgrounds with completely different perspectives on the world.
>
> The absence of different perspectives on the world is often a challenge for people who attempt to

deal with complexity. If you grew up in India, you grew up hearing three languages. You watch movies in multiple languages. When people in the Western world talk about introducing diversity, people from the Eastern world don't necessarily see that as something that you introduce, because that's what you've grown up with.

Think about it. In your own home, you've grown up with 20 different kinds of gods that you pray to, and these gods have their own little quirks, so the fact that you've grown up with ambiguity, not just diversity but with ambiguity and multiple versions of correctness, lets you deal with the unstructured barbs that are thrown at you. All of this is challenging for people who have come from societies that have regulated a lot of these things and don't expect weird things to happen to them. If you grew up in India, random stuff happens all the time! You just roll with the punches at times and know eventually how to predict where the next random thing is going to happen.

This is how Nirmalya Kumar explained it: "Most Indians can comfortably exist with seemingly contradictory worlds and ideas at the same time. Perhaps it even gives them a competitive advantage to live and flourish in a world of religious, cultural, and ethnic diversity."

And flourish they have.

To put this in perspective, there was no better person than C. K. Prahalad, who died in 2010. In one of our interviews with him this is what he observed of India's rise:

There is an old saying, I think originally in India and now everywhere around the world: it's like five blind men touching an elephant and having different perspectives. India is very similar. If you ask me whether it is world-class and an emerged country already, I would say yes if you go to Infosys, if you go to Wipro. Their technology, their governance principles, their global reach, their ability to attract talent, their capacity for innovation, make them as good as any in the world. At the other extreme, there is so much deprivation and poverty for at least 150 million people that it looks like the worst part of the world. So if you take all of India and put one label on it, irrespective of what the label is, it is likely to be wrong.

But what I would say is that in the last 10 years, India has done two things very well. One, it has built some global capabilities, first locally and then leveraging it globally, and that is where you find the IT industry, the pharmaceutical industry, the automobile components industry, the diamond cutting industry, and so on.

Second, it has created an extremely high level of aspiration for all of its people, both the poor and the rich. The rich and the educated can aspire to be world-class, and the poor can aspire to have an education for their children to allow them to escape poverty. So there is a deep focus on education. The government fundamentally accepts, even though it's very hard to implement, that India has to become an integral part of global trade. It cannot be isolationist like it is today.

So those two, I think, are going to put India on the right trajectory. In a very complex coalition, with the government at the center, India will take one step forward, half a step backward, a quarter step sideways. It is never going to be a smooth transition, and we should not expect it. But directionally, I am extremely positive on where India is going.

India has come a long way in a relatively short time. As we write, India is the third largest economy in the world, and the finishing touches are being applied to the World One building in Mumbai, which will be the tallest residential skyscraper in the world. The 117-story $400 million building will use an estimated 250,000 cubic meters of concrete and contain some 300 or so homes and a 17-floor car park.

Such achievements would have been unthinkable 20 years ago. The challenge is to apply the same ambition and ingenuity to broader social problems. According to World Bank measures, 29.8 percent of the Indian people were below the national poverty line in 2010. This is a substantial improvement from 45.3 percent in 1994.

There is still much work to be done, and the business thinkers we highlight in this book will undoubtedly play a leading role in formulating the ideas, policies, and strategies to tackle such fundamental issues.

CHAPTER
2

The Ghoshal Legacy

With his movie star cheekbones, piercing eyes, hawkish intensity, and intellectual brilliance, Sumantra Ghoshal (1948–2004) was an intimidating figure. Ghoshal held the Robert P. Bauman Chair in Strategic Leadership at London Business School, having previously taught at INSEAD and MIT's Sloan School of Management. He was also the founding dean of the Indian School of Business in Hyderabad.

Ghoshal was best known for his work with Christopher Bartlett of Harvard Business School. Their 1988 book *Managing Across Borders: The Transnational Solution* was hugely influential. In it Bartlett and Ghoshal argued that multinational corporations from different regions of the world have their own management heritages, each with a distinctive source of competitive advantage.

The first multinational form identified by Bartlett and Ghoshal was the multinational or multidomestic firm. Its strength lies in a high degree of local responsiveness. It is a decentralized federation of local firms (such as Unilever or Philips) linked together by a web of personal controls (expatriates from the home country firm who occupy key positions abroad).

The second was the global firm, typified by U.S. corporations such as Ford in the twentieth century and Japanese enterprises such as Matsushita. Its strengths are scale efficiencies and cost advantages. Global scale facilities, often centralized in the home country, produce standardized products, whereas overseas operations are considered delivery pipelines to tap into global market opportunities. There is tight control of strategic decisions, resources, and information by the global hub.

The international firm was the third type. Its competitive strength is its ability to transfer knowledge and expertise to overseas environments that are less advanced. It is a coordinated federation of local firms that is controlled by sophisticated management systems and corporate staffs. The attitude of the parent company tends to be parochial, fostered by the superior knowhow at the center.

Bartlett and Ghoshal argued that global competition was forcing many of these firms to shift to a fourth model, which they call the *transnational*. This type of firm has to combine local responsiveness with global efficiency and the ability to transfer know-how better, cheaper, and faster.

They described the transnational firm as a network of specialized or differentiated units, with attention paid to managing integrative linkages between local firms as well as with the center. The subsidiary becomes a distinctive asset rather than simply an arm of the parent company. Manufacturing and technology development are located wherever it makes sense, but there is an explicit focus on leveraging local know-how to exploit worldwide opportunities.

New Realities

Ghoshal and Bartlett's 1997 book *The Individualized Corporation* cemented their place among the world's most influential business thinkers and predicted the rise of a new organizational model based on purpose, people, and process.

The shift in emphasis in Ghoshal's work was from the cool detachment of strategy to the heated complexities of people. Whereas *Managing Across Borders* was concerned with bridging the gap between strategies and organizations, *The Individualized Corporation* moved from the elegance of strategy to the messiness of humanity.

Later in his career Ghoshal collaborated with Professor Heike Bruch of the University of St. Gallen in Switzerland to examine how the most effective managers create organizational energy through "purposeful action." Their book *Bias for Action* was published in 2004.

Ghoshal was intellectually rigorous but willing to take a stand and play an active part in debate. The new business reality as described by Ghoshal was harsh: "You cannot manage third-generation strategies through second-generation organizations with first-generation managers," he observed. Despite this damning critique of corporate reality, Ghoshal was not totally discouraged. "Look at today and compare it to years ago. The quality of the strategic debate and discussion has improved by an order of magnitude," he said. "Third-generation strategies are sophisticated and multidimensional. The real problem lies in managers themselves. Managers are driven by an earlier model. The real challenge is how to develop and maintain managers to operate in the new type of organization."

We talked to Sumantra Ghoshal in 2003.

Your work anticipates far-reaching changes in the way companies organize themselves and their resources. Does this change the way we understand management?
The dominant philosophy that has driven businesses for the last 50 years is based on the notion that a company is purely an economic entity. At its heart is the notion that ultimately the job of management is to leverage the scarce resource and that the scarce resource is capital. We have created a whole doctrine of management based on that principle.

That premise has led to a corporate philosophy based on strategy, structure, and systems. The job of the leadership is to get the strategy right and design the right structure—and tie the strategy with the structure through highly defined systems to deliver performance. That philosophy came basically from Alfred Sloan and his experiments at General Motors. But that philosophy is no longer appropriate.

What has changed?
Financial capital is no longer the scarce resource. We have seen that in recent years. We have seen trillions of

dollars chasing what is really the scarce resource today and will be even more so in the next 50 years, which is ideas, knowledge, entrepreneurship, and human capital.

This shift from financial capital to human capital as the scarce resource has enormous implications. The core management philosophy—the strategy, systems, structure doctrine—has become bankrupt because it is designed to maximize the returns on financial capital and manage financial capital. You can't manage talent and people—if that is the source of competitive advantage—with that philosophy.

What will replace it?

A very different management philosophy is arising and will become dominant—what we call the purpose, process, people philosophy.

We are moving beyond strategy to purpose, beyond structure to process, and beyond systems to people. All of this has occurred to allow the company to attract, retain, and then leverage this talent. So the management philosophy will change.

Does this fundamentally change the nature of capitalism?

I think this shift will change the basic doctrine of shareholder capitalism and moderate it so that if people are adding the most value, people will increasingly have to be seen as investors, not as employees. Shareholders invest money and expect a return on their money and expect capital growth. People will be seen in the same way. They will invest their human capital in the company, will expect a return on it, and will expect growth of that capital.

What does that mean for shareholders?

The notion that all the value is distributed to shareholders will have to change to accommodate this shift in the source of value creation. It will be a very different model of distribution that will become dominant over the next 50 years.

That sounds good in theory, but have companies really changed the way they see their people?

Traditionally people have been seen as a cost. Optimization of cost is what drove the way companies saw people. In some companies that's still the case. Gradually that view is shifting from people as costs to people as strategic resources. The company has a vision or strategy and people are a key strategic resource, so how do we align the strategic resource to achieve our vision, to achieve our strategy? At the same time, an even more radical view of the relationship between companies and people has begun to emerge: that of people as volunteer investors. With this view, it will be the individual employees who will be at the heart of the relationship; they will have to take responsibility for the development and deployment of their human capital and for the company's performance, and the company will have to play a supporting role.

What about us as employees? How does it change the way we view our work?

This is accompanied by a shift with the individual employee. Each individual employee takes responsibility for his or her own life, and that's where the people as volunteer investors fit in. They choose to invest their human capital: their knowledge, their relationships, and their ability to take action. For that they expect a return, which is indeed a return in terms of sharing the value that is created through their human capital but also to grow the human capital itself—call it the notion of employability or whatever—but to continuously grow the human capital just as owners of financial capital did in the past.

How will the day-to-day task of management change as a result of this shift?

Historically there has been a cognitive bias in thinking about management and the way it has manifested itself. When you talked about skills, we talked about the knowledge: What do you know? People were largely seen as a seam of intellectual capital.

Increasingly, what we are beginning to see is the importance of two other elements of human capital. One is social capital: the ability of individuals to build and maintain long-term relationships with other people, relationships based on trust and reciprocity. We've always known that relationships are important in business, but somehow we have not counted it in explicitly. Increasingly, what we are seeing from research is that one of the best indicators of superior performance beyond knowledge is this ability to build and manage relationships. That will become a focal point, and people will understand it as a strategic resource and companies will understand it and try to develop it.

And the other element of human capital?
The other area is action-taking ability. Companies still complain that the vast majority of managers roughly know what they need to do but that knowing what to do is one thing but most don't do it. So the ability to take action is another skill that is coming to the fore.

We are talking about the capacity to take action, the capacity to build personal energy for taking action, the capacity to develop and maintain focus in the midst of distracting events of managerial life. Action-taking ability—call it emotional capital if you wish. To sum up, historically we have seen intellectual capital as the key resource it is, but we will increasingly recognize the importance of both social and emotional capital—the development and management of relationships and action-taking ability—as the new important elements of competence that managers will need.

What challenges does that present for companies?
The moment you recognize that the value-creating resource is people, it affects everything, including how we attract whatever is the best talent in our context.

Talent is not always and necessarily the graduates of the Harvard Business School or the elite institutions. How do we identify and attract the top talent? And how do we then convert individual intellects into collective intellects? How do we link talent so that the skills and knowledge of different people can be combined to create new knowledge? And then how do we bond them to the company?

How do we create an alignment between those people and their individual aspirations as volunteer investors and the overall goals and purpose of the company? Accumulating talent, orienting talent, bonding talent—that goes right across in terms of recruitment, training and development, career path management, mentoring, right across the spectrum of people management processes. That will require very different approaches that will emerge as purpose, people, processes comes to the fore.

Does this in turn change the relationship between business and society?

Very much so. Two things are coming together. People are recognizing that to achieve superior performance the social fabric of the organization is absolutely vital even to the economic goals. To maximize wealth creation by the company, at its heart in the knowledge-based service-intensive industry is the quality of the social fabric—the quality of the social fabric, the individuals, their roles, and the relationships that connect them. That's one side.

The other side is a growing awareness that companies are the most important institutions of modern society. Much of the wealth of societies is created and distributed by companies. They are the most important actors and the profits of a society—both the economic and the social profits. Thus, companies play an extremely important role in the modern economy. With that recognition gradually the amoral notion of management—businesses only as businesses—will gradually give way to the notion of the need to align the purpose of a company with the broader aspirations of those with whom it is partnering. So both from outside and from within the nature of the social fabric will become increasingly vital and is already becoming so.

What about at the more philosophical level? It seems that the real debate about globalization is only just beginning.

At the philosophical level it has to be understood that business has to have a role that is beyond what is just the most useful for me—whether it's short-term profits or even long-term shareholder value. They have to understand that historically whenever the most important institution of the time has not understood its role, that institution has declined. That happened with the monarchy, with organized religion, and I believe it will happen to global corporations unless the leaders of those corporations recognize the profoundly important role they play in modern society and acknowledge with a show of legitimacy the social interface as an integral part of their individual and collective strategy. I believe this shift is beginning to happen.

Can globalization be a force for good?

Some people say we should all sit down together and sort it out. There is no need for throwing stones on the streets of Seattle. The trouble is that we're all caught in a catch-22. The problem for the NGOs and protesters is that the moment they are seen to work with business to solve the problems, they lose their legitimacy with their own constituency. They're caught in a catch-22. Businesses, once they lose their rhetoric, are also caught in a catch-22. We have to break this to begin a process.

There is still rhetoric on both sides—the rhetoric on the NGO side and on the side of economists and CEOs—but this rhetoric needs to give way to a recognition of the need for a partnership that benefits society for the long-term health of business itself. That debate has begun. I am optimistic that out of this direct confrontation a world will arise where a business and social partnership will occur that will be economically, socially, and morally better than the one we've seen for the last 50 years.

CHAPTER 3

Pyramid Thinking
C. K. Prahalad

Anil K. Gupta (Chapter 6) told us a revealing story. In 1975, Gupta arrived at Harvard Business School to begin a doctoral program. It was a move out of India into the academic ferment of Harvard. As Gupta arrived, another young Indian scholar, C. K. Prahalad, was leaving Harvard, having finished his doctorate. The two met for dinner.

"If I asked you the three best academics on strategy, you could tell me," said Prahalad over dinner. "But then, let me ask you, What's the name of the CEO of General Motors or Procter & Gamble? Do you know that?"

Gupta admitted that he did not. Prahalad said that knowing the leading practitioners was as important as knowing the thought leaders. It had a profound impression. "From that day on, I made it my business to keep track of what's happening in the journals and also made it my religious duty to read the *Wall Street Journal* every day and, if I had time, also *Businessweek, Fortune,* and so on. C.K. made it clear that it's as critical to read the *Wall Street Journal* as it is to read the *Strategic Management Journal.* That was with me in 1975, and it's there with me today: a love and a respect for the world of scholarship but an equal love and respect for the world of practice."

Many other academics and practitioners had memorable and fruitful encounters with Coimbatore Krishnarao Prahalad. Born in the town of Coimbatore in Tamil Nadu, Prahalad studied physics at the University of Madras (now Chennai), followed by work as a manager in a branch of the Union Carbide battery company. He then went to the Indian Institute of Management before earning a doctorate (doctor of business administration) from Harvard. He taught both in India and in the United States, eventually joining the faculty of the University of Michigan, where he was the Paul and Ruth McCracken Distinguished University Professor of Strategy at the Ross School of Business.

Prahalad's *Harvard Business Review* article "The Core Competence of the Corporation" (May–June, 1990) introduced the term *core competencies* to the management lexicon. His book *Competing for the Future*, written with Gary Hamel, became a bestseller and set the strategy agenda for a generation of CEOs.

In 2004, he published two books. *The Future of Competition,* written with Venkat Ramaswamy, introduced the notion of co-creation, and *The Fortune at the Bottom of the Pyramid* argued that the world's poor (the "bottom of the pyramid") represented an untapped market worth up to $13 trillion a year. Finally, in *The New Age of Innovation*, Prahalad continued his intellectual journey, describing a new competitive landscape that is based on two simple principles: N = 1 and R = G.

We were fortunate to get to know C.K. Whenever and wherever we met him he was characteristically generous with his time and his ideas.

You grew up in India as one of nine children. Clearly, this shaped you as a person and helped form your thinking. What did those early experiences teach you?
Growing up in India is an extraordinary preparation for management for three reasons. One, you grow up in large families, so you always have to make compromises; you have to learn to accommodate. Also, India is a very diverse culture in terms of languages, religions, and income levels, so you start adjusting and coping with diversity at a very personal level as a child.

The second point is that I was lucky because my parents were academically oriented. My father was a judge and a great scholar. He told us very early in life that there is only one thing that when you give more, you have more—and that's knowledge. That has stuck with me.

Then, in the plant in Union Carbide, I had to work with communist unions. I had to set rates—I was a young industrial engineer, and negotiating rates with the unions taught me a lot. They're very smart people, they're very thoughtful, and if you're fair and honest, you can deal with them in an interesting way. It taught me not to think of these groups as adversaries but to collaborate, be honest, be fair.

You topped the Thinkers50 in 2007, the first time that ranking has been won by an Indian thinker. It made the front page of the Times of India. *How did that make you feel?*

First, I would say anyone would be happy to be in that slot: if you're going to be in that list, it is better to be number one. But it's also a very humbling situation because if you're number one, people think you know the answers to everything. You must have the humility to say no, I don't. Therefore, I think I've become a lot more humble and, more important, a lot more cautious about what I say.

If you had to pick one theme that runs throughout your work that idea would probably be co-creation. Can you explain what it means and how it is developed in your book The New Age of Innovation?

Co-creation is an important idea. What it says is that we need two joint problem solvers, not a single problem solver. In the traditional industrial system, the firm was the center of the universe, but when you move to the new information age, consumers have the opportunity to engage in a dialogue and be active and therefore can shape their own personal experiences.

Thus, with co-creation, consumers can personalize their own experiences and the firm can benefit. This is becoming much more common and possible today.

What would be an example of that?
Let's take Google; everybody Googles now. But if I look at Google, it does not tell me how to use the system; I can personalize my own page, I can create iGoogle. I decide what I want. Google is an experience platform. Google understands that it may have a hundred million consumers, but each one can do what he or she wants with its platform. That is an extreme case of personalized, co-created value. In the new book our shorthand for that is N = 1.

However, Google does not produce the content at all. The content comes from a large number of people around the world: institutions and individuals. Google aggregates it and makes it available to me. That is the spirit of co-creation, which says that even if you have a hundred million consumers, each consumer experience is different because it is co-created by that consumer and the organization, in this case Google. Resources are not contained within the firm but accessed from a wide variety of institutions; therefore, resources are global. Our shorthand for that is R = G, because resources are now coming from more than one institution.

N = 1 and R = G are going to be the pattern for the future.

In the book, you talk about traditional industries as well as high-tech companies like Google. You also apply R = G and N = 1 to service industries such as teaching. Can you give us an example of how that would work?

Let's take the tire industry. It is a Rust Belt industry that has been around for 100 years. Selling tires to fleet owners, for example, is a well-established system. The channels are known, and the product is very clear. But imagine if instead of selling tires to a fleet owner, I decide to sell a service, tire usage. Because people drive trucks differently—some are short-haul trucks, some are long-haul—there's a wide variation. So I say I will charge you only for kilometers of usage: all that I have to do then is measure how many kilometers each truck travels.

Then I can go one step further and put some sensors on the tires so that I know the tire pressure, I know the braking speeds, the terrain in which you drive, and so on. And with a Global Positioning System, I can also see what routes you take. Now I have a much better understanding of how you use the tires. Therefore, I can now tell you to please check your tire pressure and rotate your tires, because tire pressure and rotation can dramatically improve usage and reduce the cost for you as a fleet owner. The sensors on the tires give me a tremendous amount of knowledge about how people really use the tires or run their vehicles.

And the tire seller and the fleet operator are co-creating value that way?

We're co-creating value. But I can go one step further: say you have 500 drivers. Now let me take Joe as one driver, and I can look at his driving habits and give him advice on improving safety and tire usage to make him a better driver. Thus, what used to be an arm's-length transaction, mostly based on price, can be converted into a personal relationship with a driver and a relationship with the fleet owners so that I provide extraordinary service and get compensated very well. I also get tremendous ideas for product development, because now I have real-time data (not data from focus groups) coming to me. That is the kind of transformation all firms can go through.

What does that sort of transformation mean for the way managers think and act?

Managers must shift from a firm-centric view in which the firm is the critical unit of analysis to accepting the centrality of the individual consumer as the critical unit of analysis. That's a very important first transition.

Does that apply across the globe? Is the thinking relevant in China and India and other cultures that aren't quite so individualized?

Actually, I think everybody wants to be treated as unique. We all want to have an opportunity to express ourselves. I believe less industrialized societies, emerging markets, can move there directly. They don't have to go through the process that the West has gone through. For example, think about telephony: Why should they go through landlines before they go to wireless? They don't have to go through the same process of getting old television sets before they go to plasma TV; they can go directly there, and the costs are going down anyway. One of the things that I'm arguing is that N = 1 and R = G works across the globe.

More important, when people are connected around the world, they want to have the same things. They don't want to be treated in China and India as if they're still in the Stone Age or at the beginning of the industrial age, where you get what we produce for you. Suddenly, in the United States and Europe, you can get highly personalized experiences. Why can't we create the same individualized experiences worldwide?

So there appears to be a paradox here, because at the same time that people want the same things, they want them to be unique—uniquely their own things.
That's right. Therefore, the first principle that managers need to grasp is the centrality of the individual. The second principle is the interdependence of institutions, that you do not try to do everything yourself. The reality is that you cannot; even if you're IBM or GE or P&G or Unilever, you still have to depend on a large number of other institutions. Therefore, in this new world, ecosystems compete, not individual companies. There's the second principle, the R = G.

The third, which is even more interesting, is how value is created. The traditional way of thinking about value creation was as a value chain that was captured by the supply chain. Value was created and captured in a product, which the consumer paid for. In this traditional type of transaction, the consumer played no part in creating the value. But if the consumer is involved in co-creating value, you have to recognize that in your pricing. You have to recognize that a portion of the value is created with the consumer at the point of interaction. You have to take account of that in the way you price and charge for that value. That is the third transition.

Do you think that most managers find these transitions daunting?

These are not difficult transitions, but they are hard to do in one leap. You must have a point at which you aim to transform your company. But that doesn't mean you have to go from A to B in one fell swoop; you can migrate systematically. So I say small steps, directionally consistent steps, are what companies need to take.

We've talked about management. But what do these new ways of thinking mean for the way we lead? How do they change leadership?

I would say there are three very important distinctions. First, leaders must lead. You cannot lead unless you're future-oriented. Leadership is about the future, leadership is about a point of view about that future, and leadership is about hope.

*That's the first point. And the other changes
for leaders?*

The second point about leadership is that it's not
about the leader. The metaphor I like to use is that of
a sheepdog, not a shepherd. A sheepdog has to respect
some rules. Number one, you always lead from behind.
Number two, you can bark a lot but don't bite. And
number three, don't lose any sheep.

In other words, a leader is somebody who can
bring out the best in you, not the best in himself or
herself. That is a very different view. It's what Gandhi
did. If you really think about Gandhi, looking at him,
looking at his physical stature, looking at his clothes,
nobody would have said he would have left a fundamental imprint on human history. But he was a
great innovator; his leadership was about change, it
was about hope, it was about freedom, it was a very
personal thing. He made every Indian realize his or
her own personal ability to contribute to that effort.
And very importantly, he set some nonnegotiables.
It was not an armed struggle; it was a peaceful struggle, and that was nonnegotiable. So that would be my
third principle: some things are nonnegotiable. Moral
authority comes from having clear nonnegotiables.
And that takes courage.

So for me leadership is a point of view, the ability
to mobilize people and make them achieve their very
best and to have moral direction. It's not only technological capability and economic strength; it's morality
as well.

*The Fortune at the Bottom of the Pyramid discussed
how business, including big business, can actually
work with emerging markets and in doing so alleviate
some poverty. How does that fit with your ideas about
innovation? Are these ideas all linked?*

I think they're very closely linked. Actually, my last
three books—*The Future of Competition*, where the
co-creation idea was born; *The Bottom of the Pyramid*,
looking at 5 billion underserved consumers; and *The
New Age of Innovation*, with the N = 1 and R = G
idea—are parts of a larger argument. But I had to separate them into bite-size concepts so that the message
didn't get confused. But now I've told you, and you
can see how they fit together.

If you look at the opportunity for companies,
I'm making three simple points in all three books.
One: look at 6 billion people as your market, not just
the billion at the top of the pyramid. Look at 6 billion people as potentially microproducers, microinnovators, and microconsumers. Today companies are
starting to say we want to straddle the pyramid, not
only be at the top, not only at the bottom, but we can
take our products to all. You see this with a company
such as Unilever: whether it's Dove or Sunsilk or any
of its other branded products, Unilever is looking for
ways to make them affordable all the way from the top
to the bottom. We can package it in a sachet for poor
people in India who can afford only a small quantity at
a time, and for more affluent buyers, we can give them
big bottles, if that's what they want, at the top of the

pyramid. Straddling the pyramid is becoming a fairly common idea.

The second thing I'm saying is that if you want a good way of serving the consumers and therefore retaining consumers, you have to understand the uniqueness of each one and create a unique personalized experience. That means you cannot just give them a product and think of the relationship as a transaction. You have to build a relationship that is more enduring. That's the whole co-creation idea.

Third, in *The New Age of Innovation*, I'm taking these two ideas and then saying, How do you do it operationally? What is the glue? The glue is information architecture, or IT architecture, and the social values that you create are the social architecture in terms of skills, training, approach to talent, and so on.

So they all come together, and I believe that we are on the verge of the largest growth opportunity that any firm has ever seen. Just imagine: even if you don't take 6 billion people as your market, if you can just go from 1 to 3 billion, that's still the biggest growth opportunity people have ever seen. I think we are on the verge of something extraordinary.

Beyond the Pyramid

In our final interview with C.K. in 2010 he had recently been reconfirmed as the world's leading business thinker, topping the Thinkers50 for the second consecutive time. We discussed the success of *The Fortune at the Bottom of the Pyramid*.

Were you surprised at the impact The Fortune at the Bottom of the Pyramid *has had?*

In an interesting way I was. The thinking around the world before the book came out was that the poor are wards of the state. They need help; subsidies are the way to go. And so there had been a whole range of efforts by developmental economists, multilateral institutions, aid agencies, and philanthropists that had gone on for 50 years. To be able to come and say there may be another way of solving this problem was quite radical.

I was never sure whether it was going to be an acceptable thesis, but surprisingly, multilaterals, many NGOs, and a lot of companies have come to accept this. Aid agencies now ask, Are we creating a market-based system? Can we create transparency? Can we build capabilities? From that point of view it was a big surprise.

The second surprise for me is that although ideas like core competence and co-creation have all become part of the lexicon, it took a fair amount of time. But bottom of the pyramid (BOP) has become part of the lexicon in a very short period. That is also good news. Five years on, I am surprised how many companies have small initiatives going and are starting to understand how to participate.

It was 2004 when you first published the book, and you are now publishing a new edition five years on. What's changed since then?

If you look at what has happened since the book, three questions that everybody had in his or her mind have been answered conclusively. Is there a real market? Can you make profits? and Will the poor accept new technologies? The revolution that wireless has brought, with 4 billion people connected in the world, has proved that all this is possible. Certainly the poor are accepting new technologies, whether it's in sub-Saharan Africa, southern Africa, Indian villages, Latin American villages; people accept new technology. They are finding new applications. There is a huge market. Just in India they are getting 11 to 12 million new mobile phone subscribers per month, not per year but per month, demonstrating that if you hit the sweet spot suddenly, this market is real, and most important, companies are making money, whether it's Cell Tel, Safari.com, Airtel, Reliance, or Globe in the Philippines. All of them are making money, and more important, the market capitalization of these companies is real. There are four companies in India that didn't exist 15 years ago and that now have a market capitalization, in a depressed market, of $45 million. Thus, those questions are being answered.

More interesting for me are suddenly iconic innovations like the Tata Nano, which is creating an inflection point in the global auto industry. Now, a $2,000 car does not mean that all poor people can afford it, but maybe in India not a billion people but 300 million people can aspire to this. Tata Nano actually received $600 million in advances so that people can take delivery of the car in 2011. Now, that is an interesting perspective on the global auto industry. Everybody is shutting down plants, giving concessions to people to buy cars, but in India people are giving Tata money so that they can get delivery in 2011. There is something that is happening in this market that we ought to be sensitive to as managers, as practitioners, and also as academics.

In the new introduction you explicitly talk about the democratization of commerce. Can you tell us exactly what that means?

I start with a broad philosophical perspective. The twentieth century was about political freedom. I recognize it is still a work in process. We are not there, but people recognize political freedom as a birthright. So now I ask myself, What is the big challenge for all of us in the twenty-first century? It's how to democratize commerce.

Think about core competence as an idea. Core competence is not about top management. It's about ordinary workers, ordinary people, and the worker community working together to create intellectual capital. It is essentially saying don't underestimate the critical value added by ordinary people. It's not all about the top guys. Now the idea is widely accepted.

Then you move to the second idea of co-creation. Co-creation is about saying, How do we empower consumers? How do you empower both suppliers and consumers so that collectively we can create more value? Connecting with suppliers is now called connect and develop, or open innovation, but this idea has not suddenly happened. It is an old idea. Co-creation with consumers is happening all over the place, and *The New Age of Innovation* is all about how to make it happen.

I want you to think—that's the core competence idea. I want suppliers and consumers to think with me—that is the co-creation idea. Then if you put the two together and go to the bottom of the pyramid, you are essentially saying, How do I get all people in the world to have the benefits of globalization as consumers, producers, innovators, and investors?

Think of the world as a combination of micro-consumers. That means you have to make things affordable, accessible, and available. As microconsumers we also want to exercise choice; that's co-creation, and that applies across the board. Even if you can afford what only rich people can afford, you still want to co-create. Personal choice and affordability are two sides of being the consumer. The idea of democratization is building systems in which you as a person can be a microconsumer, microproducer, microinnovator, and microinvestor.

Connectivity allows ordinary people to connect, disintermediating the tyranny of large institutions, and that is an important innovation taking place right in front of our eyes. Look at what happened in the 2008 U.S. presidential campaign. It was all small contributions, not just the big blockbuster donors, and that made Obama successful.

Democratization of commerce forces us to think about three issues in a very important way. First, there is the centrality of the individual rather than the institution. Then there is the interdependence of institutions. Nobody can do this alone any longer. It doesn't matter how big the company is. That's why even companies like Procter & Gamble have to think about connect and develop. Everybody now understands that. That means you have to compete as an ecosystem. The third issue, which is more important, is iterative, interactive innovation, which involves a large number of people.

A lot of things in life can be small steps taken very rapidly by a large number of people, creating big change. You can see what has happened with Facebook, Twitter, and LinkedIn. These are fundamental changes taking place rapidly, seamlessly, and painlessly. Nobody is forcing you to be part of it, but you see the benefits of being part of it. I think we are on the verge of this new intellectual, organizational, and social challenge of finding a way to allow everybody to participate in the benefits. That does not mean everybody gets to be equally successful, but everybody has the right to participate and opportunities to participate. At least that is my hope about where we are going.

People such as Bill Gates are talking about creative capitalism. Is your vision very different from his, or are you converging on the same ideas?

No, actually it is not. I think it's an important debate. You get creative capitalism, you get capitalism with a conscience, then you get social capitalism or social innovation. You get creating shared value, stakeholder capitalism. I think the new forms of capitalism connect two things. First, they connect fair markets. Transparency is still important. Fair evaluation of value is still important. Second is co-creation. We collectively have to understand what value is. So if you connect markets, which is economic understanding, transparency, access to information, and elimination of asymmetry of information, you get the idea of co-creation, you get democratization.

Through all this noise, the underlying signal is very clear: we are becoming more interdependent, we recognize it, and the markets are becoming more important as a way to solve complex problems. I think democratization to me is bringing the two together.

Does that require a new type of leader? What are the characteristics of the leaders who are going to lead in this new era?

I think humility is a good start. I think we got to a point where if you wanted to be a leader, you had to be arrogant. No. I think leadership is about hope, leadership is about change, and leadership is about the future. If you start with those three premises, I want leaders who are willing to listen and bring in multiple perspectives, because the future is not clear.

Finally, I would say leaders of the future will have more moral authority. It's not hierarchical authority. If you think about Ghandi, he did not have big armies. His force was moral force. The virtue in Ghandi was that he was never dogmatic. He was tough, he was autocratic many times, but he was willing to change his methods. People listened to him. Now, he was not always the most democratic person, but he listened to a lot of people, and he had clear values.

The last time we saw you, you said that what we need to think about is the next agenda for humanity. Would you like to answer your own question?

What are the fundamental drivers of a social order? Globalization is one of them. The second, which is big for me, is how to create inclusive growth. That's the bottom of the pyramid: how to get 5 billion more people as microconsumers, microproducers, microinnovators, and so on. The third big piece for me is how to empower people. That is co-creation. The fourth one is that suddenly if you have 4 billion new consumers and producers, the earth will be in a situation that is not sustainable. We all know that. Already it is not very sustainable.

I look at it and say 1.5 billion people have created this problem, and when you have 6 billion people, there are only two choices. One is to tell them not to come out of the village, not to enjoy the basic amenities of life. If the additional 4 billion people represent only 10 percent of energy consumption that you and

I have, it's almost like adding the whole of the United States again, 400 to 500 million new energy equivalents of the United States. It's not possible. To me the next big challenge is how to look at sustainability not as compliance and regulation but as a fundamental requirement for innovation.

If I want to make cataract surgery available at $30 rather than $3,000, I have to innovate. That's exactly what happened in the bottom of the pyramid. So we have to bring the same energy for breakthrough innovation to sustainability. Think about a model where you have inclusive growth, sustainability, co-creation, and globalization creating interdependencies. Putting all these things together and thinking systematically about them is the next challenge.

Reinventing the BOP

Sadly, C.K. is no longer with us, but we are thrilled to report that his legacy lives on.

Indian thinkers continue to lead the way with ideas that address the issues that C.K. cared about. BOP thinking is being applied in new ways to new challenges.

The work of Bhagwan Chowdhry, a professor of finance at UCLA's Anderson School, is a powerful case in point. A meal with Vijay Mahajan, India's father of microfinance, led to Chowdhry and his host coming up with Financial Access @ Birth (FAB).

Behind it are some striking facts. As Chowdhry points out, nearly half of the world's adult population has no access to basic financial services. At the same time, more than half of all births in most developing countries go unrecorded. Unregistered children are likely to be among the poorest and most socially marginalized members of society. Those without a legal identity find it hard to obtain even the most basic services, such as bank accounts. They are also disadvantaged when natural disasters and conflicts occur as attempts to distribute water, food, and medicine are often compromised by corruption and the inability to identify recipients.

Together these facts make a compelling case for a new way of thinking.

As Chowdhry explains: "These intertwining circumstances led me to found the Financial Access @ Birth initiative, which aims to place $100 in an electronic savings account for every child born in the world. The bank account will be integrated with a birth certificate and universal ID when those forms of identification exist. The initiative is based on incentives: $100 will persuade parents to register their child's birth, and a bank account will encourage savings and asset building. Eventually mobile phone access will make it easier to transfer cash to those in need.

"A deposit of $100 also incentivizes banks and financial institutions to become more inclusive. A long-term stable deposit account is a bank manager's dream, and although the account size may be small, our estimates suggest that it is sufficient to make FAB accounts attractive."

Banking with a social conscience can only help improve the sector's reputation from a very low starting point. Best of all, we like the FAB idea because it makes sense from all sides. It is microbanking for mutual gain. Chowdhry calculates that banks' interest and fee income would exceed their funding cost by 4 to 5 percent annually.

It is a hugely ambitious project. We liked it so much that in 2013 FAB was short-listed for a Thinkers50 Distinguished Achievement Award—an award we are proud to call the C.K. Prahalad Breakthrough Idea Award. (Also nominated in the same category were Navi Radjou and Subir Chowdhury, who are featured later in this book.)

It is telling that three of the six short-listed nominations were for Indian-born or -educated thinkers not because of where they come from but because of where their ideas are taking us. C.K. would have approved.

CHAPTER
4

Making It Happen
Ram Charan and
Subir Chowdhury

There is something inspiringly pragmatic and adaptive about many of the Indian thinkers and corporate leaders we have met. This was brought home to us when we met Vivek Singh, CEO and executive chef of the Cinnamon Club group of restaurants in London.

In the late 1990s, Singh's career in India was well set. He was working at the Rajvilas Hotel—72 luxurious rooms set in 32 acres of land. And then, by chance, Singh encountered Iqbal Wahhab, a Bangladeshi-born Briton who had launched *Tandoori* magazine in the United Kingdom and was then in the process of developing ideas and raising capital to launch what would become the Cinnamon Club. He and Wahhab kept in touch, and eventually Singh was persuaded to become the first chef of the Cinnamon Club.

"Iqbal said to me, I'm trying to open this restaurant, and I want it to be like no other. So I said, What are your thoughts, what are your ideas? What are you trying to do differently? And he said we will have the most amazing room—12,500 square feet! No cloth wallpaper; I'll have the best service, good china, good cutlery, crockery, and so on. I said, What else? And he said well, what else do you think? And I suggested a completely different sort of food that combined my knowledge of Indian recipes with a wider range of ingredients. I knew the 300 or so Indian recipes but was looking for more."

Naive Cuisine

Vivek Singh arrived in London for the first time with his team of five chefs in December 2000. "All the people who worked with me moved. It was a journey, an exciting change from doing a certain kind of cooking that everybody else was doing to something that only we would be doing." On March 21, 2001, the Cinnamon Club opened its doors to the public.

The commercial, culinary, and personal risks were substantial. Singh had never previously visited the United Kingdom. Now he was involved in the launch of a restaurant right in the heart of London that was making claims to revolutionize the eating experience. "In many ways ignorance is bliss. I never really thought about whether it would succeed or not. Naivete! I had nothing to lose," says Singh. "I wanted to cook; I wanted to do more and more. And the more you do, the more you want to do." There was a lot to do. In three months Singh had to figure out the groundbreaking food to accompany the groundbreaking customer experience. He had to discover suppliers in a strange city and much more.

When the new restaurant was launched, Singh was totally immersed in his work. His memory is of recipes, ingredients, menus, spices, the kitchen, and little else. "I had a small stake in the business, which kind of just washed over me, because I wasn't interested in a stake in the business. It wasn't what I was focusing on. I was focusing on the excitement of creating a new menu. But it was intense, so intense that I don't really remember much of that period. A kitchen is a kitchen. If you are there for 14 or 16 hours a day, it doesn't much matter if you are in Jaipur or London."

For the first six months, Singh and his team worked seven days a week. They routinely started at 8 a.m. and finished at midnight and beyond.

The Shock of the New

For some, experiencing this new take on Indian cuisine for the first time was undoubtedly a shock. "I am sure there were some people who didn't like it, and Iqbal must have been told it wouldn't work and so on," Singh recalls. "It was very pure and undiluted on my side. It was very haughty. We stuck to our way. We were isolated, dogged, and thick-skinned, but six months in we were gaining credibility. The thing is the British love curries, but they also love experimentation."

Experimentation was what they got. Now into his culinary stride and lauded as groundbreaking, Singh could have paused for breath and enjoyed the plaudits. Instead, he decided to change the menu every day. The bar was raised. "One of the older guys I'd hired locally came to me and said chef, it's none of my business, but with due respect, you've got to be careful with what you're doing. You're putting everything out; one day you'll run out of ideas, and then there'll be no value. And they'll get rid of you. You're young, you're enthusiastic, I totally respect all of that, but you don't need to change menus every day.

"Actually, the more you create, the more ideas you have. Whenever we meet, we often talk about it, and he says you were right. By creating new dishes, you never run out of ideas, you come up with more new ones. And I think that's what we found and our team finds as well. The challenge now is to meet expectations. Now commercial success is also on the agenda as part of those expectations. We are constantly innovating, never standing still."

The Peripatetic Coach

Such restlessness is second nature to Ram Charan, one of corporate America's most respected executive educators and consultants. In a career spanning more than 35 years, he has worked closely with some of the world's best-known CEOs, including Jack Welch during his time at General Electric.

Charan started his business career working in the family shoe shop in India. He went on to Harvard Business School, where he gained an engineering degree and then an MBA and a doctoral degree before becoming a member of the faculty. In 1978, he left academia to establish the Dallas-based consulting firm Charan Associates.

Famously peripatetic, Charan teaches at corporate executive education programs and consults to the boards of Fortune 500 companies. At GE's famous Crotonville Institute, he won the Bell Ringer (best teacher) award. He has received similar accolades from the Wharton School at the University of Pennsylvania and at Northwestern's Kellogg School of Management.

A prodigious writer, Charan is also the author or coauthor of a number of influential books and articles, including the 2002 bestseller *Execution: The Discipline of Getting Things Done*, with the former CEO of AlliedSignal Larry Bossidy and Charles Burck; *Boards at Work; What the CEO Wants You to Know; The Leadership Pipeline*; and *Every Business Is a Growth Business*.

Would you describe yourself primarily as a teacher, a consultant, or a writer?

Neither. It is a mix of things I do. I teach on the executive programs of companies. I facilitate at the top management level for off-site events, and I also do corporate governance work. The reason you have difficulty pigeonholing me is that most people have one silo and I was lucky enough to see the issues that general managers face. My main focus is strategy, leadership, organization, and the board.

You are better known inside corporate America's boardrooms than outside. Is that a deliberate choice?

I have avoided publicity. It is only recently that I began to write books. My reputation is based entirely on word of mouth. That means you have to contribute every day. So wherever you go, people have to see value every time they work with you. The value comes from converting ideas in a way that is useful to the companies I work with. The distinguishing characteristic is that I'm not going there saying here are some tools, what are your problems? I'm going there saying let me see what your problems are and how can I help you? That's the difference.

You've been described as peripatetic. But how much time do you actually spend on the road each year?
I'm on the road 100 percent of the time, and this is my twenty-sixth year.

Do you ever come home for long periods?
I have an office but no home. I book into a hotel wherever I happen to be.

But your office is based in Texas. How big an operation is that?
A secretary.

Your work has a very practical focus. Is that because you do a lot of hands-on consulting?
I was teaching at Harvard and Northwestern when I formed my ideas. Most of those ideas are difficult to translate into practice. I look at the situation, the industry, and the global economy factors and develop a specific solution. Most of these theories really are impractical.

Other thought leaders seem to approach the world with a ready-made theory, which they then apply to a situation. Are you saying that you do the reverse?

I first want to find out what the issues are that a company is facing—what are the challenges?—and then work through to the solutions, which is the most rewarding part.

You encourage executives to think like a street vendor. Why is that?

Every company listed on the FTSE or the New York Stock Exchange has to answer the same basic questions: What's your margin? What's your growth? What's your inventory turns? What's your cash flow? What do you know about customer needs? Why do you succeed against competition? They are the same business questions that a hawker has to understand. If you master the relationship between these things, that is the nucleus of any business. Then you have to learn how to scale it up. So whether you are GE or Toshiba or any other company, it's exactly the same thing. But if you don't master the nucleus, you will have difficulty mastering the scale.

Is running a big company such as GE fundamentally different from managing a shoe business in India, or is management universal?

There are universal questions—the ones I mentioned earlier. The difference is scale, complexity, and the sheer size of the organization. That's a huge difference.

But when it comes to final decisions they all have to match the same five or six things.

Execution, the book you coauthored with Larry Bossidy, is subtitled The Discipline of Getting Things Done. *But isn't execution inseparable from management rather than a discipline in its own right?*

That's a good question. What we are saying is that lots of people talk in terms of theories, and visions, and missions, and strategies. They use terms like *high-level*, but getting it done requires something more. There is a discipline, a routine, tools you can use to achieve flawless execution. But that cannot be done without leaders and managers mastering that discipline.

What's the key difference between companies that have an execution culture and those that don't?

Everyone talks about culture, but if you don't operationalize it, it doesn't actually happen. Culture is not enough. Leaders have to drive execution, but you have to go down further and say, What are the various processes in the company that combine to create the culture? Which of these processes is working, and which is not? What is working to deliver financial results, and what is not working? Then how do you improve those processes that are not delivering results—what is your execution methodology? This book lays out the methodology.

Doesn't that lead to a company that is focused on numbers to the exclusion of everything else?

No. What you find is that over time it comes down to the orientation of the people side—the social system. That's where a lot of businesses fail. The contribution of this book is that it links the numbers and the social system. That's crucial.

You've worked with a lot of business leaders over the years, including some big names. What do you regard as the most essential attributes for a modern CEO?

Everyone has his or her own theory. But in my opinion the key here is that if you have a long-term CEO or leader—someone who has been in the job more than four or five years—the most critical skill is selecting the right people for the right jobs. That is more important than strategy. The other part is choosing which direction to go in. These two things are critical.

Another area of your expertise is CEO successions. Why do so many CEO successions fail?

There are two major causes. One is that in most companies that pretend to have succession planning the succession planning process is bankrupt. It is politically highly charged, and there's a lot of history. But there is no useful dialogue to calibrate it, and that's why it doesn't work. In many companies there is no succession planning. These are the two major reasons.

In IBM, for example, there was fantastic succession planning in the 1970s and 1980s, and it failed to produce a successor, and so an outsider was brought in.

The flaw in that system was that it did not pay attention to identifying businesslike, profit and loss type genes. Therefore, it did not succeed. Lou Gerstner comes in—he knows what he's doing because he's done it at American Express. He's able to rearchitecture that, and he produced a successor from within IBM.

In most cases companies are forced to bring in someone from outside because the company's situation has deteriorated so badly. Before Gerstner arrived, IBM had come very close to disaster.

You've also written a lot about why CEOs fail. Are they failing for the same reasons today or are there new causes?
The main reason is the same. It is failure of execution.

We also have more CEO failures. Why is that?
If you're not training these people and you're not selecting them properly through succession planning, what do you expect? Business schools don't train for leadership. They train for tools and techniques and frameworks. No business school can train leaders. Leaders are trained in the military, in sport, in the political arena, and through work. But business schools have been incapable of producing leaders.

Is that a great failing of business schools?
They don't claim they are creating leaders. They select leaders and give them some tools. So it's not a failing.

They are very clear about it. The best training is still the military. It is the job of companies to develop leaders: to give them experiences of leadership and then assess them and rate them and then move them. Companies have to do that, and most companies have not. Why would you expect not to see higher failure rates?

The other thing that has happened here in many cases is that when companies select leaders, they get seduced by intellectual capacity. Intellectual seduction means they appoint a very bright individual who makes great presentations. These people appear to be able to really get their arms around the issues, but when it comes to getting things done, they don't have the necessary skills.

Most books on leadership use the same examples:
Jack Welch, Richard Branson, Winston Churchill, and
so on. How helpful are these role models?
I have worked with Jack Welch for a long time. What you can learn from people like that is the tools they use, what approaches they use, what they think helped build success. That's different from using him as a role model. There are no two Jack Welchs; there are no two Winston Churchills or Richard Bransons. But there are some ideas, techniques, and tools.

Someone who wants to emulate one of these leaders is likely to fail. Anyone who likes to learn one or two things from successful people, including these leaders, is likely to get something out of it.

Does Jack Welch have a good grasp of what made him successful?

I've known the man for a long time. If you read his book carefully, he says it is the selection of people. And he was very clear about where to take the company. Those are the major pillars of his success. It's all there in his book. These two things can be learned.

Quality Matters

Another Indian thinker with a healthy obsession with execution is Subir Chowdhury. For him the key to effective implementation is adherence to the principles of Total Quality Management, something that he argues can play a vital role in leveraging resources and eliminating waste at an individual, organizational, and even national level.

Chowdhury is chairman and CEO of ASI Consulting Group. Tagged the "The Quality Prophet" by *Businessweek*, Chowdhury is the author of *The Power of Six Sigma: An Inspiring Tale of How Six Sigma Is Transforming the Way We Work* (2001) and 11 other business titles.

His book *The Ice Cream Maker* (2005) is a business novella about Pete and the ice cream factory he manages. The book follows Pete as he improves his business by applying total quality principles; the book was distributed to every member of the U.S. Congress.

The Power of LEO: The Revolutionary Process for Achieving Extraordinary Results (2011) explains how organizations can harness Chowdhury's listen, enrich, and optimize concept to make quality part of their DNA.

Chowdhury studied for his bachelor's degree in aeronautical engineering at the Indian Institute of Technology (IIT) in Kharagpur and earned his master's in industrial management at Central Michigan University.

Can you tell us about the golden thread that runs through your work?

Over the last 20 years I have worked on the area of process quality. Essentially, quality is the combination of people power and process power. When you talk about process power, it's very simple. It doesn't matter what industry you are in: healthcare, manufacturing, the service industry, or government. If there is work, there is a process. If there is a process, there is variation. Variation means sometimes you do well, sometimes you do badly; sometimes the process can be faster, sometimes the process is not doing what it's supposed to do. My expertise is all about how to reduce the variation, because variation is the reason waste happens, and when waste happens, it affects the bottom line.

When I go to organizations, it's not about fixing the posts; it's trying to teach the correct tools so that they can make the process as perfect as possible, relieve the waste, and save money.

Then around four or five years ago I noticed that some companies using my process were getting much better returns than others. That raised the question of why, using the same process, one company is getting 100× and another company is getting 10×. It bothered me, and I questioned myself. Maybe I'm not a good teacher, maybe my organization isn't helping these clients, maybe our own process is wrong.

We went back to the drawing board and figured out the main reason this happens. Initially I challenged my colleagues, and they said every organization is different and maybe we should study our clients. So we studied the clients, and what we found out was that in the companies receiving a 100× return the majority of the people from the bottom all the way to the CEO level have a quality mindset. But in the companies only getting a 10× return they do not have that top to bottom quality mindset.

Before you can teach process quality, you have to make sure the people who are applying that process also have the quality mindset. I have come to realize that it is the mindset part that makes a big difference. That is the reason Toyota was successful when its competition struggled. Toyota has a quality mindset culture.

Then it occurred to me that I should teach the common masses about the principle of quality in language that anybody can understand. I thought about how I could take this statistical jargon and turn it into a language that everyone can understand. So I wrote the ice cream maker book. If I give that book to a politician, he or she will understand it. If I give the book to a schoolteacher, he or she will understand it; even the schoolchildren will get it. Even if you give it to a fifth-grader or a sixth-grader, he or she will understand.

If your mindset is "quality belongs to me and I can make a difference," you are already 50 percent of the way there because you will have that continuous improvement mindset.

How important is your message in a country like India?

Very bluntly, one of the major problems in India is corruption and waste. If you visit India right now, you will be completely blown away because corruption is still there the same as 50 years ago. It might even be worse now because people became even more money-hungry, and they are going after the money rather than going after what they are passionate about.

In my view India cannot solve the corruption issue as a nation if it does not have the quality mindset.

Is India making progress with this?

The quality message sounds very good in a *Financial Times* or *Wall Street Journal* article. It may convince Westerners, but it's very different on the ground.

If you visit India now, you will find a lot of places, big, big signboards saying ISO 9000 certified, Six Sigma certified. The sad part about that is that it sounds good on the surface, but if you go deep into how they achieved that certificate, they might have achieved it by giving bribes. Society cannot improve by doing that, and even though I may sound politically incorrect, that is a fact.

For example, if you go to some of the hospitals, the way they treat patients, the patient's life is not the number one priority. How much the patient is paying or his or her family's ability to pay the money is more important.

That is not a quality mindset. But if you go to any Western country, in contrast, whether you have money or not, when the emergency happens, they will not ask you if you have the money. The first job will be to try to save the life of the patient, and these are very fundamental issues.

India doesn't have a monopoly on corruption, though. It's not just India, of course. Even if you think about Dr. Deming and some of my own mentors, all of their lives they talked a lot about process quality, but in our field, unfortunately, nobody really preached about the people quality part. Even in the financial crisis and everything else, even if you think about it either in Europe or in the United States, there is so much corruption that happened, even in the richest of the rich. They also had corruption over here in the United States. I'm not suggesting that the West doesn't have these issues. They have corruption too, but if you don't have a quality mindset, it will have a much bigger economic impact on the nation.

Even though I am still helping corporations on the process quality side, right now I am much more focused on the people quality side. These are the two areas of my major expertise.

You are now applying your ideas about quality at the national level. Can you explain that?

I'm making an argument that poor quality, either the people quality or the process quality, has a huge economic impact on a nation. Think about a country like England, where you are. England used to have amazing brainpower, and it still does. So the question is: Why has England lost tremendous amounts of competitive advantage? And the answer, in my view, is that England did not concentrate on quality. I firmly believe that, and even in America right now, America is going down a little bit for the same reason. I call it an American disease: they do not have that quality mindset.

For example, think about government, either the U.K. government or the U.S. government. Forget about India, China, and those; I'm just talking about Western governments. They have spent trillions of dollars. But if I ask you what percentage of government dollars are being used efficiently, you will be very lucky if they don't have at least 50 percent waste. So in any project, it doesn't matter what department, half of the money will be wasted. If it is only 50 percent waste we will be lucky. Thus, while the U.S. administration—any U.S. administration—spends billions of dollars on any project, 50 cents on the dollar is being wasted. That's waste, literal waste.

You're talking about the economics of quality, the idea for which you were short-listed for the Thinkers50

Breakthrough Idea Award in 2013. How do you define it?

The way I define the economics of quality is in terms of the economic impact that results from that waste. To put it another way, it is the unrealized economic impact that results from not applying the process quality. Let me give you a real example. The U.S. Defense Department has a budget to develop a next-generation aircraft. They have spent, I believe, close to $20 to $30 billion, and that aircraft is supposed to serve both the navy and the army as well as the air force.

All three armed forces were involved in product development, but when the product came out, none of the three wanted it. In the process, $20 billion has been lost. Right now, they are still trying to figure it out because it's stuck in their throat. They cannot swallow it, they cannot throw it up, so they have to figure something out.

Now, think about that part: $20 billion of the taxpayer's money! How can that happen?

And it's not just defense.

Defense is just one example. Think about the wasted economic impact in any healthcare area or job creation scheme. A couple of years ago some economists advised the U.S. president to spend a billion dollars for every state. The idea was that if you gave every state a billion dollars, then $50 billion of jobs would be created. So a billion dollars was given to every state, and then what they found out is that out of the billion dollars maybe

$300 or $400 million is left unspent. Do you know what they are doing? Because that money has to be used within three months, they are breaking up good roads and then fixing them so that they can use that money.

Is there any way of quantifying how much is being wasted?
Billions and billions of dollars. But the question is, What can be done about it? The problem is that the economists who advise governments don't know how to resolve this issue.

I have spoken to Nobel Prize–winning economists about this. These economists advise the president, and the president is listening to their advice. The problem is that economists can tell me what is good and what is bad, but they don't know how to transform bad into good. No economist seems to know how to transform a bad product into a good product, a bad process into a good process.

The sad part is that they are advising on the basis of economic models. I don't have any problem when the economists suggested giving $1 billion to every state. No problem. But the economists should have said to the president that when you give the money, you must demand 90 percent efficiency. But they do not know how to create a quality mindset and quality processes.

I'm trying to blend the topic of quality and economics because I'm trying to tell them that if you don't demand efficiency, you will not get the expected economic impact. That's at the macro or national level, but economics of quality also has an impact at the community level.

Can you give us an example of that?
I am involved with some research at the London School of Economics, and there is some brilliant research one of the students has done. There is one particular area in India that has specialized in textiles for generation after generation. They are phenomenal in textiles. They produce textiles.

What the research is finding out is that in that area, little by little by little, the fine quality of textiles is going down and down. The question is why. He started with what's happening in that village, and what he found out is that a lot of the textiles workers have cancer. A lot of them are suffering, and the next generation is suffering because they pass the techniques from generation to generation. So a lot of them are dying at the age of 45 to 50, that sort of age. Then he found out that the same river that is the only source of their drinking water is also where they wash the textiles. Thus, it's a process problem.

Literally on one side of the river they are washing textiles, and on the other side of the river they're bathing and using it as drinking water. It is completely polluted. It's a human tragedy.

What can be done about it?
The researcher became very passionate about this, but the local government didn't give a damn, and

forget about the central government. Central means the federal government in India, and they didn't give a damn about it. Then what happened is that the researcher was selected as a London School of Economics fellow.

Once that happened, I pushed him. I said look, you can write academic papers about all this stuff, but that will not help. What you should do is write a column in the *Economic Times of India*, but you have to write it in the *Economic Times* language and talk about it this way, and then the awareness will come. Because you are a London School of Economics fellow, they will listen to you. They will talk about it and say hey, look, this is the research that's been done.

Finally he is getting some traction, and the local government and the central government are getting involved because they want to save that industry.

You are originally from Bangladesh, but you were educated in India. To what extent do you think that your roots in Bangladesh and the time you spent in India have affected your thinking?

I was born in Bangladesh as a Hindu boy. As you know, in Bangladesh discrimination is based on religion. India, Pakistan, and Bangladesh are divided on the basis of religion, and the sad part is that when independence happened, it's not like 100 percent of Hindus lived in Bangladesh or India and 100 percent of Muslims lived in Pakistan. It didn't happen that way. Pakistan still has 8 to 10 percent Hindus and

India still has 10 percent Muslims, and Bangladesh also has 10 percent Hindus.

So did I face some kinds of challenges in Bangladesh? Absolutely, yes, but on the other hand, if you ask me, some of my best friends in Bangladesh are Muslims. The advantage of what happened to me was that when I came to America, it became a piece of cake. Even when I faced some form of discrimination in America, it became so easy for me because I had faced a similar type of challenge, even a worse challenge, in Bangladesh.

How did moving to the United States affect your mindset?
The difference for me versus my son born in America is that because I was born in Bangladesh, because we were the poorest of the poor at that time, the only weapon I had was my education. My dad gave me only one thing, and that was education. So when I graduated from the Indian Institute of Technology, that education, that feel of IIT, the graduate of IIT, the thing I got from the school was that you can change the world. If you can dream, you can change the world, but how big your dream is, is in your hands.

So when I came to America, I was dreaming big because I believed in America on the day I landed. And when I was dreaming big, I wanted to change the world.

What is your message for the managers of the world?
My message to the managers is what I talked about in three simple steps, and obviously it will come back

to quality. I think that any manager in any position, it doesn't matter what organization, should practice three things every single day. Practice what I call listen, enrich, and optimize.

Listen to your family. Family can be your children, it can be your loved ones, a spouse, whatever it is. Listen to internal customers. Listen to your employees. Any manager, subordinate, or your bosses, listen to them very carefully. Our society is much more into talking rather than listening. Try to listen.

Once you develop that skill of listening to the internal customer, listening to the external customer will become 10 times easier. If you fail in internal customer listening, you cannot succeed with external customers. You cannot satisfy external customers if you have tension in your home; you cannot be successful externally. Listen to internal customers as well as external customers.

Everybody pretends to listen to external customers, but ideally they cannot listen because their internal customer listening is wrong. That is the most important element, listening, if they can develop their skill of listening.

And the other two steps?

Number two, enrichment. When I talk about enrichment, it is much more like continuous improvement, but again, I talk about trying to enrich your community. Try to enrich your family. Try to enrich a friend's life. If you do that, you can enrich your company, but if you fail, if you have no involvement in your community, if you don't have any involvement with your family, you cannot enrich the organization. That is the second thing.

And the third step?

The third thing: optimize. Optimize means at least try to have the perfection mindset. That means that if you believe that perfection is not achievable, you can never achieve anything. John F. Kennedy decided that America would be the first to land on the moon; that is the reason America landed on the moon. If he did not have the dream, it could not have been accomplished. If all managers could have that perfection mindset and really believe in it, they could achieve it.

Practice these three elements: listen, enrich, and optimize. If they can literally practice this, they can be 10 times more effective managers, and in the process they will add value and literally practice quality. If they can practice these three things, that means they are practicing quality. They are changing society for the better. That's my advice. This applies to any manager in any organization: it can be healthcare, in politics, in any organization.

CHAPTER
5

Innovation
Indian Style
From VG to Jugaad

"Most companies don't lack for ideas. What happens is they mistake creativity for innovation. Innovation has little to do with how creative you are. Innovation is about commercializing creativity. As Thomas Edison, the great innovator, pointed out, innovation is 1 percent inspiration and 99 percent perspiration. Inspiration and creativity are what people get wrapped up in (and there are a lot of ideas in companies!), but the 99 percent perspiration is what they forget," reflects Vijay Govindarajan.

Govindarajan, known as VG, is the Earl C. Daum 1924 Professor of International Business at the Tuck School of Business at Dartmouth College in New Hampshire. His books include

Reverse Innovation, *Ten Rules for Strategic Innovators,* and *The Other Side of Innovation,* all written with Chris Trimble.

In 2008, Govindarajan took a leave of absence from Tuck to join General Electric (GE) for 24 months as the company's first professor in residence and chief innovation consultant. At GE, Govindarajan worked with CEO Jeff Immelt to produce the *Harvard Business Review* article "How GE Is Disrupting Itself" (September 2009). The article, written with Immelt and long-term collaborator Chris Trimble, introduced the concept of *reverse innovation,* in which, contrary to conventional expectations, innovation takes place in emerging markets and then is brought to developed countries. Reverse innovation was later rated by the *Harvard Business Review* as one of the 10 big ideas of the decade.

In August 2010, Govindarajan (with Christian Sarkar) posed the question in an *HBR* blog post: How do you create a well-designed, safe, and affordable house for the world's poorest people? The result was a global quest to design a $300 house, an idea that won the Thinkers50 Breakthrough Idea Award in 2011.

Before joining Tuck, Govindarajan was a member of the faculties of Harvard Business School, INSEAD, and the Indian Institute of Management Ahmedabad. He received an MBA with distinction and a doctorate from Harvard Business School. Before that, he qualified as a chartered accountant in India, where he was awarded the President's Gold Medal for obtaining the first rank nationwide.

When we spoke with VG, we started by talking about the idea that emerged from his work with GE.

You wrote an article for Harvard Business Review *with Jeff Immelt and your associate Chris Trimble. It marked a significant change in perspective on the entire process of innovation. What was the big idea behind that article?*

Historically, global companies innovated in their home markets, the developed world, and took those products into developing countries. We wrote about *reverse innovation*, which is doing the opposite: innovating in emerging markets and then bringing those innovations to developed countries. That's the opposite of *glocalization* (a hybrid word formed by merging *global* with *localization*), the big idea in the 1990s, which has been defined as "thinking globally and acting locally."

Did glocalization simply stop working?

The reason glocalization worked historically is that American companies were taking their products into Europe and Japan, where the customers were similar to U.S. customers. That approach does not work in emerging markets because the whole market structure and the customer problems are so fundamentally different. For example, take the GDP per capita in two countries, the United States and India; there is no product in the United States, where the mass market per capita is $50,000, that can be adapted and sold in India, where the mass market per capita is $800.

Can you give us an example of this phemonenon at work?

An interesting example is GE's ultrasound machine. In the United States, the ultrasound machine looks like an appliance. It's huge, it's bulky, it costs anywhere from $100,000 to $350,000, and it can do very complicated applications. But 60 percent of India, for example, consists of poor rural areas where there are no hospitals. Therefore, patients can't go to the hospital; the hospital has to come to them. That means you can't use those bulky machines; they must be portable. Customer affordability is different as well, and so the charges people pay in the United States for an ultrasound would be unthinkable in rural India.

And this led to reverse innovation?
In short, GE created a portable low-cost ultrasound machine, somewhere in the neighborhood of $15,000, a fraction of the cost of the bulky U.S. machines, and that has opened up a huge market in China and India. The same portable ultrasound machine is now coming to the United States and creating new applications. This is a great example of reverse innovation.

It would seem this might provide GE with a chance to grow its business in India as well?
Most multinational companies, such as GE, have tried to sell their U.S. products in poorer countries such as India and China, but again, there was a serious mismatch in possible applications and pricing. That means they were capturing only 1 percent of the opportunity in those countries. But going forward, those countries are going to represent a huge

growth opportunity. In fact, I believe that in the next 25 years the biggest growth opportunity for multinationals will be customers in poor countries. That is why reverse innovation is important to GE and similar companies.

This raises a lot of fundamental questions for corporations worldwide. For example, where will companies be doing their research and development in the future?

The biggest change for American or European multinationals will be to shift the center of gravity to where the innovation will take place. That means it is an organizational challenge. You have to put the resources where the opportunities are. That means you have to localize product development, you have to localize sourcing, you have to localize strategic marketing capability. This probably represents the biggest required shift in mindset for the leaders of multinationals.

How long has GE been consciously practicing reverse innovation?

It's a relatively new concept. I would say it has caught on within the last 5 years. Although India and China opened their borders in the last 15 years, it's really only in the last 5 years that we have seen Western companies developing products that are based on what emerging markets need, want, and can pay for.

Despite this example, there isn't much of a sense that every major corporation is moving in this direction. What's holding them back?

Probably the biggest problem for reverse innovation being adopted in large companies is the companies' historical success. Glocalization, or taking global products and selling them with some adaptation in local markets, requires a fundamentally different organizational architecture, and the more you succeed in (and dedicate most of your corporate resources to) glocalization, the more you are going to find it difficult to do a good job in reverse innovation. That's probably the biggest bottleneck: historical success. Companies will move in this direction as more success stories evolve, such as the portable low-cost ultrasound machine.

Did GE encounter such bottlenecks in its own organizational culture?

Yes, without question. Here's a case in point: five years ago, under GE's glocalization model, the main responsibility of the head of GE Healthcare in India was to distribute global products. If he had to come up with a new concept to solve Indian consumers' healthcare problems, he had to do it on weekends, because he was busy selling global products during the week. But even if this health chief had written a proposal during the weekend, he had to sell it to the global product head sitting in Milwaukee, who probably had never visited India or understood the problems of its rural residents. Even if he could convince the global product head, there were a whole lot of others he also needed to convince. Thus, implementing reverse innovation represented a huge organizational challenge.

What changed at GE? What does it take to move a company toward reverse innovation?

As is so often the case, the key issue was the need for a cultural transformation, and it had to start at the top. To his credit, Jeff Immelt, chairman and CEO of General Electric, regularly visits India and China and expects the CEOs of various businesses to visit them as well. When Immelt sits with the premier of China and talks to him about key national priorities, he gets firsthand knowledge about the possibilities in China. That kind of understanding developed by CEOs is the starting point for bringing about a cultural shift. It was Immelt who demonstrated the need for GE to adopt reverse innovation, and then he encouraged the organization to catch up to his vision on this.

Do American business leaders have Immelt's vision? After all, one of the most startling statistics of our global era is that only 25 percent of Americans have passports.

Point taken. Increasingly, Western business leaders must recognize that they have a different role now inside their companies; they have to create a new global mindset inside their organizations. I think big companies whose leaders have global mindsets will be able to win in this new era in which the opportunity has shifted from developed markets to developing markets. You see, 15 years ago, when companies thought of global strategy, they thought in terms of Europe, the United States, Japan, and the rest of the world. Today and going forward, they have to think about their global strategy in terms of their strategy for the BRIC countries (Brazil, Russia, India, and China), the Middle East, Africa, and the rest of the world. The "rest of the world" has become the United States, Europe, and Japan; that is the mindset shift that will enable all business leaders to think as GE now does.

And once they do?

You've identified what is probably going to be the most significant challenge for American multinationals. They have a lot of talent, but does that talent have a global mindset? I say the biggest challenge for Americans and other multinational CEOs is to embed that mindset.

Do you think this will become Jeff Immelt's legacy?

One of the remarkable things about General Electric is that it is a hundred-plus-year-old company, and the only way a company can survive that long is if it obsoletes itself in terms of products and solutions. This is the real hallmark of GE: that it is willing to change, it is willing to embrace new ways of competing. To that end, every effective CEO puts a new strategic frame on the company he or she leads not because the old frame was irrelevant but because it's a new environment, it's a new world. The strategic frame that Immelt is putting in place (without losing the performance and discipline that Jack Welch put in place) is adding innovation to supply. Immelt's legacy will be judged by how well he was able to incorporate innovation inside a company known for efficiency.

You have a unique role inside a modern corporation: professor in residence. How did that happen?

About 10 years ago I gave the keynote address at a conference at which Susan Peters, the chief learning officer of GE, was also a speaker. I really enjoyed her talk, so I congratulated her on it. She in turn asked me what kinds of things I work on, and I told her about my work on reverse innovation. About five years later, I met Immelt when he gave the commencement speech at Dartmouth College, where I have been on the faculty of its Tuck School of Business for some time. I had a half-hour meeting with him during which I told him about my work in innovation. So when Immelt and Peters were talking about bringing in an academic to push their thinking, my name came up. It was kind of a series of fortunate accidents, and I think very few academics get this kind of an opportunity.

How would you explain what your job at GE entails?

My role consists of three things: to teach, guide, and consult. I teach the top 600 officers of GE about the best thinking in innovation. The difference between the guiding and consulting parts is that I work more deeply on a few projects when I consult, whereas when I guide, I am talking to a number of GE executives about issues on their plates. There is no typical day. That is the beauty of this work with GE. It's been probably the most intellectually challenging growth opportunity I have had.

Did that surprise you?

What really surprised me is that I never thought that one person could have an impact, particularly on a large company such as GE with its 300,000-plus employees. Amazingly, I found that as an outsider, I have some strength that an insider does not have even though I don't have a big title there, I don't have a big budget, and I don't have a big business to run. I think I can make a difference at GE mainly because I am coming in as an academic; people know that my viewpoint is unbiased.

Might you be tempted to take on a full-time GE role if offered? Do the big titles and budget tempt you at all?

Actually, this role has only convinced me that I don't want those things. As the saying goes: those who can, do, and those who can't, teach. I can't, so that's why I started teaching. In some sense, if you become an insider, I believe you lose your power base. As an outsider, you have no ax to grind, and therefore people listen to you, whereas an insider does not have that luxury.

Sounds like you have stayed true to your roots.

All people's formative years are important in guiding them and shaping them. My grandfather was a huge influence on me, and his biggest influence was to lift my ambition. He really made me believe that I could do anything that I dreamed of, so to speak. So he inculcated that ambition in me, and I think that is what probably has carried me all the way here, even to this GE opportunity. I could have been comfortable as a college professor, but just stepping into GE really lifted me to another level.

By Jugaad!

New inspirations for innovation come from unexpected places. Take what is called jugaad innovation and its key promoter, Navi Radjou. A fellow at Cambridge Judge Business School, where he is the former executive director of the Centre for India & Global Business, Radjou is coauthor (with Jaideep Prabhu and Simone Ahuja) of *Jugaad Innovation: Think Frugal, Be Flexible, Generate Breakthrough Growth* (2012) and (with Prasad Kaipa) *From Smart to Wise* (2013). He won the 2013 Thinkers50 India Innovation Award as well as the 2013 Thinkers50 Innovation Award.

What is the big idea behind jugaad innovation? It seems to have emerged very suddenly.

The idea behind jugaad innovation is to provide an alternative to the traditional model of innovation that is most prevalent in the West. If you look at the approach to innovation in developed economies such as the United States, Europe, and Japan, for the last 50-plus years the formula has been pretty much standardized. Essentially, it is a big R&D budget and fancy R&D labs. It takes many, many months and sometimes years to come up with what researchers believe are awesome products. But many of them flop in the marketplace.

The fact that you invest in big costly R&D projects doesn't make you innovative, let alone successful. This became even more important after the economic crisis that began in 2008, when companies were strapped for cash. That's when we began to look at a different model of innovation that will continue to help companies come up with new products and services but will be more affordable and more sustainable as well.

We ended up looking at the emerging markets as an inspiration for this new model of innovation. In particular, we looked at India, where the economy is very complex and there is widespread scarcity of resources. What we discovered is that even though there is a lot of resource scarcity in those emerging markets, people are resourceful. They tap into something that is abundant within themselves: their ingenuity. Jugaad in a nutshell is that resilient ingenuity that people tap into to come up with very frugal products and services that deliver greater value for their fellow citizens at lower costs. These frugal solutions include a fridge made entirely of clay that consumes no electricity, a low-cost portable infant warmer for premature babies, a mobile service that lets you send and/or receive money without having a bank account, and an advertising billboard that converts air humidity into drinkable water. The list goes on and on.

This is a new approach to innovation that we think is very frugal, very sustainable. It is also very agile because you get products and services out very quickly, and it's also inclusive because you can bring value to a broader segment of the community, many of whom might be traditionally marginalized in the economy.

And the actual word, where does the term jugaad *come from?*

Jugaad is a word from Punjabi, one of the many Indian languages. Literally, it describes a makeshift vehicle built by villagers using whatever parts they can find. It's like a Frankenstein kind of thing in which the back of the vehicle is a bullock cart and at the front of it there is a tractor engine. It's a way of transporting people from villages to cities whenever they have to go to cities. It is basically an ad hoc vehicle made up of spare parts cobbled together.

Jugaad, then, is the ability to not reinvent the wheel all the time but to see what you already have around you and then make the most of it.

Does jugaad translate easily into English or other languages? It feels peculiarly Indian.

Do-it-yourself, or DIY, is probably the closest English expression. In social sciences there is a very famous term that was introduced by Claude Lévi-Strauss, the famous French anthropologist, in the 1960s. He called it *bricolage*, and that term has been picked up in several Western business schools and used as an ad hoc translation of or equivalent to "resourceful improvisation." DIY or bricolage would be a Western term for this notion of jugaad. The growing Maker Movement in the West embodies this resourceful DIY spirit.

Jugaad is a great concept and your timing appears to have been perfect. But how do you go about actually finding companies practicing the theory?

It was a very interesting coincidence or confluence of different factors and people coming together. In my case, I started my career in the United States in late 1990s as an analyst at Forrester Research, helping Western companies become more innovative. In the early 2000s I began to pay attention to what was happening in India, particularly the innovative services offered by IT service companies such as Tata Consultancy Services and Infosys. As a regular visitor to India, I started interacting with dozens of innovative entrepreneurs and corporations there during each visit.

That was when I connected with the Tata Group, which at that time was beginning to develop the $2,000 Nano car. To be candid, initially I didn't view the Nano as an innovation because of the dominant Western innovation model in which I was trained. I had studied in France, a country famous for its scientific, R&D-driven innovation, and everything I knew about innovation was challenged in emerging markets such as India, where I saw people with very few resources who were able to come up with a lot of clever solutions such as the Nano.

Initially I dismissed the Indian approach and solutions such as Nano as low-cost stuff that couldn't qualify as innovation, but then I began to rethink what innovation really means. I realized that what matters with any innovation is that it actually creates more value for people. That's really the point, and from that perspective, a lot of the frugal solutions that are developed in India and other emerging markets do bring a lot of value for the local community.

That was when I realized the need to formalize this frugal and flexible approach to innovation because one of the challenges in emerging markets is that there is a lot of untapped tacit knowledge. They have been doing jugaad for centuries, if not millennia, and so they don't really see what's so interesting about it that is worth studying and sharing with the rest of the world. But for me, as a researcher with a global outlook, I was very excited and thought this was exactly the doctor's prescription for our resource-constrained world.

As I began to study the jugaad phenomenon, I joined Cambridge University in 2009 to launch the Centre for India & Global Business with Professor Jaideep Prabhu at Judge Business School. The Centre gave us a platform to rigorously study the new innovation models and practices in emerging markets and bring them to the Western world. Jaideep became my partner in this journey. We were soon joined by a third protagonist, Dr. Simone Ahuja. Simone was a film producer and was making a documentary on grassroots innovation in Indian villages. I was an advisor for her film. That's how the three of us connected.

We ended up forming a nice triad: with my consulting background, I brought in practical experience, Simone brought in great right brain capabilities such as storytelling and design sensibility, and Jaideep brought in academic rigor. That's how we combined these individual qualities to co-create our book *Jugaad Innovation*.

We can see that finding examples of jugaad innovation among smaller companies and in Indian communities is relatively easy. But what about larger companies? We suspect bigger Indian companies have more of a jugaad orientation than their Western competitors.

That's correct. Jugaad is more of a mindset than a methodology, and that frugal and flexible mindset is prevalent and manifested across companies of all sectors and all sizes. It is used by not-for-profit as well as for-profit companies, grassroots entrepreneurs in the tiniest villages, all the way to big corporations such as Tata Group and subsidiaries of multinational companies such as Siemens and Unilever operating in emerging markets such as India.

Do you see jugaad innovation being put to work in other emerging economies? And is it something that would really work in the West?

We will come to the West in a minute, but jugaad is definitely practiced in many other emerging markets. Africa and Brazil particularly are the closest, and China as well. In Africa they call it *kanju,* and in Brazil it's called *gambiarra.* The Chinese call it *jiejian chuangxin* (frugal innovation). China is often accused of copying Western innovation, but there is now a big push by the Chinese government to come up with indigenous innovation inspired by local needs that creates greater value at a low cost for Chinese citizens.

Jugaad is also quite prevalent in China in terms of the way local entrepreneurs and companies can quickly come up with new products and services by being very frugal and agile in how they develop solutions. Similarly, in Africa you see a lot of similar jugaad kinds of approaches such as using a bicycle to recharge a cell phone. What's fascinating is that more and more multinationals are now radically changing the way they innovate in emerging markets such as Africa by adopting this kind of jugaad mindset.

My favorite example is IBM. Researchers in the brand-new IBM lab in Nairobi, Kenya, are doing something fascinating that for me is really jugaad. It is a combination of low tech and high tech. They are taking in data feed from low-resolution webcams that track the traffic conditions in Nairobi streets and then analyzing the data by using high-end software algorithms to predict traffic jams and optimize traffic management. For me that's a fantastic example of jugaad innovation because you take what you have, which is these low-resolution webcams, and rather than upgrading them, which is expensive, you start with that and you say this is all we have, and then what can I add on top of that, which is these software algorithms, which are developed cost-effectively by IBM's army of programmers.

That combination is creating an amazing solution that is much more affordable for Kenyans than if they had to go for a very high-tech solution.

In the West, of course, we see jugaad taking off thanks to this whole Maker Movement with the 3D printing and the technology-led DIY philosophy of creating and reusing the objects we own. My hunch is that the jugaad revolution in the West might be more technology-enabled. Whereas in an emerging market jugaad is a bit more of a low-tech kind of movement, in the West it might be fueled by these emerging DIY technologies, such as 3D printing, which is becoming democratized and more affordable.

As these DIY technologies become more widespread and are integrated with social networking tools, they will provide a platform for everyday citizens to unleash their ingenuity in a collaborative way. In both emerging markets and the West, however, the philosophy of jugaad is the same. It's all about tapping into one's ingenuity to improvise creative solutions, except that the tools might be a bit more high-tech in the West than in emerging markets.

To some extent perhaps we are already seeing this with apps where small developers use their ingenuity to develop apps at a low cost. Technology is opening up new jugaad frontiers!

Yes, that's already happening. Smartphones are becoming the new platform for "maker" entrepreneurs to develop affordable hardware solutions. Take CellScope, a start-up that is a spin-off of Berkeley University in California. CellScope has created accessories that you can attach to your iPhone and convert your smartphone into an otoscope or dermascope. If your kid is complaining of some ear problem, you just plug it in the ear and see if there is an ear infection. You don't have to go to the hospital, and so it saves you time, and that attachment costs a fraction of even the lowest-end device used by a physician. In coming years, I see the smartphones becoming a cost-effective hardware platform for developing all kinds of very affordable solutions in industries such as healthcare that need them the most.

So, if someone reading this interview works for a multinational corporation, what are the takeaways for them?

First, I think we need to bring back the principle of KISS: keep it simple, stupid. In the West we have a tendency to make things complex. Our current R&D philosophy is, Why make things simpler when you can make them more complex? The first lesson is that we have to move away from what I call a just in case engineering mindset to a just in time engineering approach that yields good-enough solutions. Let me explain what I mean by that. It has been reported that many features in Microsoft Office applications are never used. Microsoft engineers overloaded Office with features just in case users would need them some day—but they never did! Instead of creating a good-enough solution with the features that users need the most, Microsoft ended up producing this monster Office software that is too bloated, expensive, and complex to use. They need to switch to a just in time design approach by asking: What is the strict minimum set of features that users really need so that they can immediately get the most value from the software? Then you focus on delivering just that, and later you can incrementally add more features to the software as required.

And, can you give us an example of that?
Salesforce.com is a great practitioner of this just in time design approach: they dynamically add (or remove) features on the basis of massive real-time customer input. The lesson in that regard is: don't initially launch a too-complex overkill solution because you are going to alienate a lot of users. Start with something simple, frugal, or good enough, as we call it, and then iteratively improve it. That's one key lesson.

Are there other takeaways for executives?

The second lesson is partner, partner, partner. I think one reason companies in emerging markets are so good at innovating faster and cheaper is that they rely heavily on third parties. They go deep into local communities and co-create solutions with many local partners. Large Western companies think they can do everything in house.

I would say open up and engage suppliers, your local community, as co-creators rather than trying it on your own.

And the third takeaway?

The third message with the jugaad mindset is around leadership. Leaders need to create space and time for employees to innovate—a playground where they can play. Google does that well. Jugaad, for me, has a childlike magic in it. Remember that *ingenious* sounds like *ingenuous*, which implies innocence and a sense of wonderment.

Employees are able to come up with the most innovative solutions when they are not encumbered by the rigid processes and structures of companies. Large companies are too uptight right now, and the only way they can loosen up is by converting the workplace into a playground. One company that has done this very well is Ford. They have partnered in Detroit with TechShop, which provides a maker platform, to repurpose a warehouse as a big playground where Ford employees can go in their spare time—evenings and weekends—and toy with 3D printers and other DIY technologies without any constraints. It's a playground where they can do whatever creative projects they want.

Through that process, Ford engineers are able now to come up with really innovative ideas that otherwise they would not do inside a formal R&D lab where there are more restrictions. Thanks to this initiative, Ford has managed to increase the amount of patentable ideas by 50 percent while reducing its R&D spending by a significant percentage. Literally, they can now innovate much more with a lot less.

That for me is the third big takeaway: jugaad happens only in a very messy environment. The more processes you put in and the more structured the environment is, the more innovation becomes very incremental. People take only small steps and keep watching their backs. But when employees are given freedom to think and act like kids in a playground, they don't give a damn about rules; they just go and play and try to break the rules. That's how you get disruptive innovation.

Innovation has become too serious within corporations. We need to rekindle its playful side. Companies need to bring back the magic and fun element of innovation.

Where does your work go next?

I'm very excited because I'm working on two big projects that are both related to jugaad. First, I am curating a big exhibition sponsored by a large European firm. It is an exhibition that will celebrate human ingenuity in its purest form. We will show how in the developed as well as the developing world everyday citizens, entrepreneurs, and visionary companies are innovating in a frugal, flexible, and inclusive manner to come up with affordable and sustainable solutions that address the most pressing needs in our societies. This exhibition will be launched in Paris in late 2014 and then will travel all around the world.

I'm very happy to bring this kind of optimistic message to the masses so that they can be inspired to use their own ingenuity to solve pressing problems in their local communities.

The second big project I'm working on is a book on frugal innovation, a sequel to *Jugaad Innovation*, but this time focusing more on the developed world. This new book will show how even wealthy economies—such as the United States, Europe, Japan, South Korea, Singapore, and Australia—are adopting frugal innovation to address the needs of cost-conscious and environmentally active citizens.

We have some very, very cool case studies of companies doing frugal innovation, especially in France and Europe, and that's something that baffles me. I have spent the last 15 years in the United States and have seen a lot of the big ideas in the past coming from here, such as open innovation. P&G is an American company that pioneered open innovation in 2000. But interestingly, this time around I feel Europe is way ahead of the United States in the practice of frugal innovation. That's exciting for me because I am a French national and have been collecting amazing case studies on European pioneers of frugal innovation, whether it's Pearson, Unilever, Siemens, or Renault-Nissan; the list goes on and on. I am really perplexed to not have found yet any large U.S. company really doing frugal innovation, although there are a growing number of entrepreneurs in America who are doing it.

That worries me because I admire American companies and have always viewed the U.S. economy as a global trendsetter. But lately I worry that U.S. companies are not thinking big enough. I feel they have become a bit too complacent. If so, they have to be careful because they may be missing out on frugal innovation, which is a megatrend that is starting to emerge. U.S. companies, especially U.S. multinationals, have to look at what's happening not only in dynamic emerging markets such as India and Africa but also in what they call Old Europe, which I believe is finally reawakening.

CHAPTER 6

Global Voices

Pankaj Ghemawat and Anil K. Gupta

Along with new ideas about organizational architecture, emerging micromarkets, and innovation, the best Indian management thinkers bring a new perspective on globalization. From a purely Western vantage point, the world can seem very flat, but to those with one foot in the developed world and the other firmly rooted in the developing world, the picture appears more complex.

Having made the journey from their homeland to the West, many of the Indian thinkers we have met are keenly aware that globalization has different connotations depending on the place where one experiences it. It can be an opportunity or a threat. It can also be overstated.

Globalization 1.0

One Indian thinker challenging received wisdom about the world is Pankaj Ghemawat. Nominated for the 2013 Thinkers50 Global Solutions Award for his Global Connectedness Index, Ghemawat is based at New York's Stern School of Business and IESE Business School in Spain. Before that he was the youngest full professor ever appointed at Harvard Business School.

His book *World 3.0* won the 2011 Thinkers50 Business Book Award. Best known for his work on globalization, Ghemawat also has written *Games Businesses Play* (1997), *Creating Value Through International Strategy* (2005), *Redefining Global Strategy* (2007), and *Strategy and the Business Landscape* (2009).

In *World 3.0: Global Prosperity and How to Achieve It* (2011), Ghemawat examines globalization and the assumptions made about it. He refutes the idea that there is a single global economy, the central premise of Thomas Friedman's 2006 book *The World Is Flat*. Instead, he argues, on the basis of various economic measures and indicators, nations are much more disconnected than we imagine. We live, he says, in a semiglobalized world at best.

Regional differences exist and matter, argues Ghemawat, and the unevenness and differences that exist from region to region are a potential source of commercial advantage. We talked to him about his perspective on globalization.

Your book is called World 3.0. *The assumption being that there was something wrong with World 1.0 and 2.0.*

Well, let's start with World 1.0. When I was in graduate school, I took a whole course in macroeconomics from Martin Feldstein, and what he told us on the last day of the course was, well, it's great that you've absorbed all these models, but these are all closed economy models, and if you want to take advanced macroeconomics, that's a whole different kettle of fish. So that to me is World 1.0, recognizing that there are cross-border interactions but still pretending that we can more or less grasp reality by thinking of countries as self-contained.

And from World 1.0 we then moved into World 2.0?
World 2.0 is actually still with us. This is the belief that is the polar opposite of World 1.0; it states that national borders don't matter at all and cross-border integration is nearly complete.

That's the Tom Friedman view that the world is flat?
I ran a survey recently on the *Harvard Business Review* web platform giving people three different worldviews that they could sign up for, and 62 percent of the respondents went for Friedman's characterization of a world in which borders don't matter, distance is irrelevant, languages have no effect, and so forth.

You argue that the world isn't as flat as Friedman would have us believe.
Right. I think most people would recognize that there are still some barriers, but it's amazing to me how many people regard those barriers as just noise or trivial, as witness the responses to the *HBR* survey I

mentioned. What I'd like to do is get people to focus on countries of particular interest to them and try to really understand the structure of those countries' international economic relationships. Take the United States, for example.

The largest bilateral trading partner of the United States isn't China; it's Canada. Canada is also the largest supplier of oil to the United States. Canada also ranks in the top two countries in terms of destinations for U.S. citizens placing phone calls. Yet Canada is certainly not the second largest economy in the world.

International phone calls actually account for only 2 percent of total phone calls, which is shocking to people who believe in a globalized world.

The basic point is that these levels of cross-border interactions are much lower than what you would expect in a fully integrated world, and they are also much lower than what people tend to guess. This suggests that it's important to recalibrate and start with an accurate picture of how integrated we actually are, and that's what I try to present in *World 3.0*. We are actually in a state of semiglobalization. What you find is that only 10 to 25 percent of most types of economic activity are international. Even more surprisingly, the lion's share of that activity is between countries that are similar: share borders, belong to the same trading bloc, speak the same language, or have colonial ties. As distances and differences between countries increase, their economic interactions typically decrease.

Yet a lot of people are very frightened of globalization. Why are people so scared of it?

I think it goes back to exaggerations about how globalized we actually are. If you're proglobalization, this is dangerous because it suggests to you that there's no further room for increases in integration to yield any benefits. And if you're antiglobalization in a 100 percent globalized world, it's plausible to blame everything on globalization. Thus, many of the fears that antiglobalizers have about globalization are fueled by the same kinds of misconceptions that lead even proglobalizers to overlook the gains from additional integration.

People are fearful about losing their jobs, they are fearful about the poorer parts of the world being exploited by the richer parts, all these sorts of things, but what you're saying is that those fears are overblown.

There are some real issues here. I spend seven chapters in my book dealing with various kinds of market failures and fears that people have and whether globalization makes them better or worse off, and I think that for some of these failures and fears you can actually see globalization ameliorating rather than aggravating things. For other failures and fears, although globalization may play a role, 10 to 20 percent globalization plays a very different role from what one might expect 100 percent globalization to play.

A tension within the book—in fact it's the central tension—is between this process of globalization or

international integration, if you like, between econo-
mies and the notion of regulation and reining it back
and, to some extent, protectionism. Can that tension
be resolved?

At the end of the day, there are some tensions, but I think the tensions do get relaxed if you've recognized how limited current levels of globalization are. Let me give you an example. What people in poor countries in particular worry about the most is food prices. In fact, I started writing this book in response to the international rice crisis in 2007–2008, when international rice prices tripled. To many people then and to many people now, this is an argument for shutting down international trade in rice.

But when you realize that only 5 percent of the rice that is produced in the world is traded internationally, you realize that anything that happens on the supply side or anything that's happening on the demand side gets loaded onto that 5 percent. The way of dealing with that is not to reduce that 5 percent to 2 percent or 1 percent; it's to increase the fraction that's traded globally. Increasing integration in this instance would actually help.

You asked about regulation, and rice is a good illustration that although increased integration can, as in this instance, help reduce volatility, it probably isn't sufficient because it's neither politically nor ethically justifiable to let people starve if they can't afford rice at the prices at which it settles down. At the end of the day, I have a message that involves certainly relying on integration as the prime engine of moving the global economy forward but recognizing that in some circumstances we will need some regulation.

What about a situation such as the production of rare earths, a commodity being used in a lot of electronic and computer devices? People point to the fact that China appears to have a global monopoly. What's the situation there?

Well, certainly China has approximately 95 percent of rare earth production. This is another kind of market failure that people worry about: small numbers or, in its extreme form, monopoly. Monopolies are bad, but it's hard to say we're the United States or we're the United Kingdom; we should shut ourselves off from the world in response to this problem. It's much more efficient to do what's being done and help other countries that have reserves, such as Vietnam, develop those sources of rare earths.

We still have a lot of monopolies, or oligopolies, particularly in commodity sectors, and the answer is not to shut oneself off from the rest of the world. With something like rare earths, if you don't have those reserves, there is no possibility of developing them yourselves. It's about trying to build up a more robust supply chain that involves more integration with more countries rather than turning one's back on the world.

World 3.0 talks about how we can respond as individuals and recognizes that we are individual units of analysis in this globalized world. Can you tell us a little about your notion of the rooted cosmopolitan?

Well, the rooted cosmopolitan is a little bit of an analogue of the country example that I was just using. Where you're located affects what's close and what's far. Rooted cosmopolitans recognize that certain experiences and certain peoples are much more approximate to themselves. A rooted cosmopolitan does not attempt the rootless cosmopolitan idea of trying to pretend that one cares equally about everything that's happening everywhere in the world. A rooted cosmopolitan realizes that we all have certain roots and that that's important in figuring out what we should try to do and with whom we should try to do it.

Are you saying that this is a more realistic notion than urging people to suddenly become global citizens, which we have failed to take on board?

That's right, and my favorite example of that is this notion of looking at the reality versus some of the rhetoric around global citizens. People who have the concept of universal cosmopolitans as opposed to rooted cosmopolitans suggest that we should care as much about people halfway around the world as we do about our neighbors, but I think both psychologically and economically that's unrealistic. What I emphasize instead in my book is that if you look at how much, for instance, the governments of rich countries spend on domestic poor versus foreign poor, the ratio is roughly about 30,000 to 1. As to what we're talking about, let's say the real target for increasing aid to developing countries is bringing that ratio down from 30,000 to 1 to 15,000 to 1. That strikes me as a much more realistic proposition than simply saying okay, that ratio has to go to 1 to 1, which is not going to happen this century or probably the next century.

Do we need a new sort of regulation? Is it time now for supernational regulation that would operate across national borders?

Governmental bandwidth is always scarce, and I think, especially given how old our multilateral institutions are, that's the scarcest kind of governmental bandwidth imaginable. Another thing that I try to do in the book is articulate which kinds of problems can be regulated locally and which few problems absolutely do require multilateral coordination and multilateral regulation. Take the problems associated with pollution, for instance. For most pollutants that have very short radii and that operate over very short distances, local or national regulation works perfectly fine. For pollutants with intermediate ranges, say, carbon dioxide, acid rain, having to do with sulfuric acid being deposited by rain, regional solutions can work and have in fact worked. Of course the hardest kind of problem is something like carbon dioxide in global warming, which isn't distance-sensitive; there we do need multilateral coordination. But rather than say that everything should be a multilateral solution, I try to specify in what kinds of cases multilateral coordination is really required because that's the kind of coordination that seems hardest to achieve.

Can we put a reverse gear on globalization, on integration? Can we actually go backward? Is this a realistic proposition?

Well, let's start with the problems in the eurozone. I think the problems in the eurozone, and it's a similar set of problems with the Schengen Area without border controls, was a focus on just administrative barriers between countries and the very naive notion that if you got rid of those administrative barriers, all other problems would be taken care of and perfect integration would result. Having a common currency did not eliminate the economic differences among different parts of Europe in terms of productivity, growth rates, willingness to work long hours, and so on.

Similarly, eliminating border controls did not eliminate the cultural prejudices that people in different parts of Europe have about people from other parts of Europe. One of the things that have to happen is recognizing that there are actually many barriers to cross-border integration and that unbalanced integration is not the way to go. Having said that, I am very worried that steps backward in terms of revocation of the Schengen accords or ejecting Greece from the common currency represent the first significant reversals of a process that's been under way in Europe for the last 50-plus years. It's a process that has proceeded in fits and starts, but compared with the original vision that the founders of the European Steel and Coal Community had, it has probably been the single most successful example of integration in the postwar period. There was some real momentum to the process, and it is disturbing that we're talking about having to take steps backward, although again, it is a reminder of the perils of unbalanced integration.

We've talked about governance, and we've talked a little about individuals. What about companies? How should companies respond to globalization and to recognizing that they're in a 3.0 world?

The first message for companies is that you actually have to recognize that differences still matter. In some senses, this is the oldest lesson in international business, yet it's a mistake that you see companies making over and over again. For instance, take the case of Walmart, which is a company I've studied for 25 years now. About five or six years ago, Lee Scott, who was then the CEO, was asked what made him think Walmart could be successful internationally, His response was in essence, look, if we could move from Arkansas to Alabama, how different is Argentina going to be? It's been quite a learning experience for Walmart that the differences between Argentina and Arkansas are a great deal bigger than the differences between Arkansas and Alabama and require much more adaptation.

It's interesting, too, that companies such as GE, which used to think that globalization was about simply exporting the same products that they made in the States, have radically changed their point of view with experience.

Yes, I think GE is certainly a company that's been in the vanguard of management thinking in a number of respects, and I think the evolution at GE is a very interesting reminder of both the distance that companies have come and the distance that remains to be traversed. In terms of the distance they've already traveled, moving as you suggest from an export-focused model to realizing that they actually need local operations, that was something that really picked up steam during Jack Welch's last 10 years as CEO, when they set about, especially in the aftermath of the GE-Honeywell deal, realizing that they actually needed to have a presence in Europe as opposed to just exporting to Europe. They're now very serious about expanding beyond Europe to Asia, which is where a lot of the growth, if you look at GE's results in the last few years, has been.

Having said that, GE is still trying to find the right managers to put in place because given the way seniority-based systems work, GE is a company that, like most large companies, derives the bulk of its revenues and earnings from outside the United States. But the overwhelming majority—90 percent by my estimate—of the top 200 people at GE are Americans. There is a mismatch there that they're working on, but it's an illustration of how much remains to be done to make GE better able to maximize the potential from operating in such different geographies.

Global Journeys

Another Indian thinker cutting a swath through conventional thinking on globalization is Anil K. Gupta. Together with his Chinese wife and collaborator, Haiyan Wang, he offers a view of the world with a fresh perspective on India and China.

Gupta holds the Michael D. Dingman Chair in Strategy and Entrepreneurship at the Smith School of Business at the University of Maryland and is a visiting professor at INSEAD. He is also chief advisor to the China India Institute, a Washington D.C.–based research and consulting firm. He is the author (with Toshiro Wakayama and U. Srinivasa Rangan) of *Global Strategies for Emerging Asia* (2012), (with Girija Pande and Haiyan Wang) *The Silk Road Rediscovered* (2014), and (with Haiyan Wang) *Getting China and India Right* (2009). He and Haiyan Wang were short-listed for the 2013 Thinkers50 Global Solutions Award.

When we talked to Anil Gupta at his office in Maryland, we began by charting his journey from being a young student in India to teaching at a leading American business school.

It's a long way from the Indian Institute of Technology to where you are now.

Yes, although actually in one sense it's not such a long way because when I was a student there, the Indian Institutes of Technology were more like Western islands within India.

Once you finished your bachelor's degree at IIT, it was common for everybody to apply for graduate studies in the United States. None of us had ever left India, but we kept ourselves, even back in those days, well informed about the United States. We had 300 students who graduated in my class. Within a year about 160 were in the United States.

I was in the top 5 or 6 percent of the graduating class at IIT, which means I was a pretty good engineer, but I somehow didn't enjoy engineering. I was good at it but wanted to do something different, I wanted to go into business on the management side, and instead of applying to graduate school in engineering in the United States, I did my MBA and initially started out with a focus on the relatively engineering-related field of industrial engineering, operations research, and so on.

In my second year of the MBA, I shifted to something very different: consumer goods marketing. When I finished my MBA, I was lucky to get one of the two most sought-after jobs in India at that time, with Unilever in India. If you were interested in marketing, which a lot of my colleagues were, the job of choice was Hindustan Lever (now Hindustan Unilever). I joined as a management trainee, did that for about 18 months, and became a product manager for some of the Unilever brands in India.

I was with Unilever for three years. Despite the fact that as a product manager you are launching two or three new products every year and so on, I didn't find it intellectually exciting.

I said I need to do a PhD and go into research or academia or maybe consulting and so on. I applied to a few schools and then joined the Harvard Business School doctoral program.

I started with marketing but shifted in the first year to strategy. In strategy I had some very good advisors. Michael Porter, Alfred Chandler, and Jay Lorsch were some of the key professors I was working with.

When were you at Harvard?
That was 1975 to 1980.

Porter was just in the early stages of his career then.
He was in the early stages of his career, but even at that time there was enough buzz around him that people were saying he is a hotshot. He was not yet a full professor, but he was clearly viewed as a strategy star.

There are a lot of strategy professors who go through their careers with very few interactions with real companies.
I don't see anything wrong with people who have a slightly different background, but I do believe that they should not get lost in the world of pure abstraction. Ultimately strategy is social science, not abstract mathematics; therefore, you need to have a pretty good understanding of the real world.

I finished my doctorate in 1980, and the first 10 years were all about hard-core strategy, building on my thesis. Vijay Govindarajan and I wrote a lot together from 1980 to about 2002 or 2003. Around 1990, I shifted my focus to globalization and global strategy and wrote *The Quest for Global Dominance* with VG (published in 2001).

This was the first major piece of my writing that was not for an academic audience. I was a chaired professor and wanted to become absolutely committed to writing for managers.

It was also around that time that I decided I needed to go deeply into the emerging market story of China and India. I was born and brought up in India, but that's not the same as knowing India analytically.

Also, 2001 is when Haiyan and I married. She is as hard-core Chinese as I am Indian. We started looking at China and India analytically and writing about them. This led to *Getting China and India Right* (2009).

Globalization remains where 100 percent of my time and energy is spent, but within globalization, there are always highly interesting new topics.

Our 2014 book *The Silk Road Rediscovered* is about the corporate linkages between India and China. It's still in the early stages, but there are a number of pioneering companies moving from India into China and from China into India. They are learning to conquer each other's markets and at the same time become globally stronger as a result.

A case in point would be Huawei, a Chinese company that has its biggest R&D center outside China in Bangalore, with more than 2,000 engineers. Similarly, in reverse we have companies such as Mahindra from India, in tractors, currently fighting for number four or number five market share position in China's tractor market with about 10 percent market share with the expectation that maybe within three or four years they could be in the top three. You would normally not think of an Indian company being a big player in China's tractor market, but it is.

These days, I also spend a considerable amount of energy and time analysing global megatrends. Over the last 20 years, from 1990 to now, the world has become dramatically different along a lot of dimensions—economic structure, technology, demographics, resources, the environment, and so forth. I believe that over the next 10 years the world will change even more dramatically than it has over the last 20. I spend a considerable amount of time looking at the big factors driving this change and what these changes mean for companies, countries, and individuals.

I have also started working on an exciting new project, currently titled "Cloning Silicon Valley." Every president, prime minister, governor, and mayor in the world wants to create a Silicon Valley. I am in the process of going deep into the Silicon Valley ecosystem and decode the factors and dynamics that make Silicon Valley the world's preeminent innovation center. I already have a fairly good understanding of Silicon Valley because I spent a year at Stanford in 2000 as a visiting professor, and so there is much to build on. After that, I plan to go deep into what's happening in Beijing's Zhongguancun high-tech park, Z-Park, the closest that China has to a Silicon Valley.

I also plan to study Bangalore, which is the closest to a Silicon Valley in India. In Bangalore, it's interesting that the government, if anything, has been an impediment rather than a stimulus or a facilitator. Bangalore has become an innovation powerhouse despite the government, Beijing because of the government, and in Silicon Valley the government is basically not a relevant factor. So, there are some fundamental differences between the three innovation ecosystems.

We will look at this global phenomenon of cloning Silicon Valley with the primary focus on the Bay Area, Beijing, and Bangalore. That's the next major project that Haiyan and I are currently working on.

What has surprised you about the rise of India?

Back in the 1970s, when India was still growing at the so-called Hindu rate of growth at 2 to 3 percent, and my student friends were applying to graduate schools in the United States, you had to take the TOEFL exam, which is a test of English as a foreign language. Only half jokingly, we used to say there will be a day when people will have to take TOHFL test of Hindi as a foreign language.

We knew that India was a large country, that the elite educational institutions were very strong, and that the calibre of the students was absolutely world class. There were some fundamental strengths, but the government was really the problem, which remains true, very much, today.

I think the surprising thing was that, instead of let's say going from 2 to 3 percent to 5 to 6 percent, India in the middle of the last decade actually started growing at 8 to 9 percent, even sometimes stretching to 10 percent. So that was a bit surprising and China-like. As I see today, the prospects are better than even that, and over the next 10 years, India's economy may grow faster than China's. Mind you, India is about 20 years behind China. As a result, India will not catch up with China anytime soon. However, it's more than likely that it will slowly but steadily start narrowing the gap.

What gets you out of bed in the morning? What's the big motivator?

For me the biggest motivator is that I see myself as an intellectual entrepreneur. Of course, when I was in India with Unilever, I had a fantastic job. MBA students would kill for that job, but I wanted more intellectual excitement than being a product manager. That has remained very true.

It's the intellectual excitement, plus I think I've always had an entrepreneurial mindset, which means that I want to be my own boss rather than have an institution or somebody else dictate, which is possible as a professor. What the university wants professors to do is to do work that they love to do and that would have impact.

CHAPTER 7

India Inc.

The rise of Indian management thinking has been accompanied by the rise of India as an economic powerhouse led by the flag carriers of corporate India. India Inc. now boasts several benchmark global brands that act as role models for companies around the world. The growing list includes the likes of Tata (which owns Jaguar Land Rover); the technology companies Wipro, Infosys, and HCL Technologies; and the tractor maker Mahindra & Mahindra.

India Inc. (along with China Inc. and some other notable newcomers) increasingly poses a challenge to the hegemony of the top Western companies. It is notable, too, that the CEO of Microsoft is the Indian-born Satya Nadella.

India Unleashed

From his vantage point at London Business School and now at Tata, Nirmalya Kumar has charted the rise of India Inc. As a marketing professor, he is especially interested in what the brand of India stands for. As with previous emergent economies such as Japan, the made in India moniker is undergoing a subtle change. This was Kumar's insight when we spoke:

> If one considers the staggering development of Indian commercial success over time, it is a magnificent achievement for a culture that was always willing to dream (and do) more. One cannot really grasp the potential for Indian business unless one also understands the roots of Indian enterprise. The rise of India Inc. can be summarized in four words: from local to global.
>
> The transformation of Indian companies from domestic to global players went through three phases. In the prereform phase, before 1991, Indian business was under shackles, first from British colonialism and later (postindependence) from socialist policies. In the second phase, post-1991 economic reforms necessitated a decade-long corporate restructuring to make companies globally competitive. Now, in the third phase, Indian companies are increasingly going global.
>
> Indian global powerhouses until recently never had the confidence or the ability to be on the world stage. Forged in India's harsh environment, these companies are now increasingly seeking to secure the best of

both worlds: access to the lucrative high-margin markets of the developed world by owning companies in Europe and the United States while maintaining their low-cost bases in India. Today, the remarkable thing that strikes one about Indian companies is that they have massive aspirations to be global companies and are extraordinarily confident about acquiring foreign firms and integrating them with their companies in India.

Although it is only to be expected that some of these Indian acquirers will stumble because they have either paid too much or taken on large amounts of debt, the overall trend remains unaffected. For the developed world and its companies, the era of India as a major overseas investor is here. The question is not how to stop this trend but how to deal with it. There was a time when Westerners assumed that an Indian in the head office of a multinational or Western company was either an accountant or a computer nerd. Nowadays that person is just as likely to be the boss.

The Art of Marketing

Kumar's career has been steeped in marketing. He describes himself as "passionate about marketing and willing to espouse controversial positions." (The other passion he publicly avows is the arts, in particular the paintings of Jamini Roy, the father of Indian modern art, and the poetry and other writings of Rabindranath Tagore, the first Asian to win a Nobel Prize.)

After earning undergraduate and master's degrees in India, Kumar completed his MBA at the University of Illinois at Chicago and his PhD in marketing at the Kellogg School of Management at Northwestern University.

Today's principal drivers of marketing success, according to Nirmalya Kumar, are speed and reach. Speed is exemplified in instantaneous global electronic communication but also in the continuous innovation of new and improved products if a company is to achieve sustainable marketplace success. Reach refers to global presence but also C-suite presence. Reach is personified in an influential chief marketing officer but also in a CEO who recognizes a role for marketing that is as critical for sustainable corporate success as are finance, operations, and information technology.

However, in today's corporate world, we find the profession of marketing in crisis. Kumar contends that marketing is "caught in the whirlpool of corporate obscurity." It is drowning in responsibilities for "tactical implementation issues" with little or no strategic influence. It is associated with the slow growth stemming from worldwide recession such that "people in marketing start losing power." Boardroom meetings include the CEO, the CFO, the COO, and perhaps the CIO, but "very few companies have the CMO . . . the voice of marketing in the boardroom."

Kumar argues that for marketing to be top of mind for the CEO, "It must become strategic, cross-functional, and bottom-line-oriented."

Becoming more strategic also involves focusing beyond survival, considering the long-term impacts that marketing can deliver as well as those in the short term. Overcoming the short-term emphasis among today's investors, analysts, and media is no mean task.

Kumar notes that marketing is more prone to short-term fixes than are other corporate offices because its key metrics are more subject to quantifiable short-term measures. The short term involves expenditures that generate sales. "There, I can show you the impact right away," he says. This is not the case, however, with expenditures on customer service, brand identity, and other spending for which "we don't have financial indicators" yet have a need to establish benefits in "brand awareness, distribution availability, looking at how much esteem the brand is held in."

Launch and Learn

Among the controversial positions Kumar espouses is his insistence that marketing in today's world requires a company to be "market-driving" rather than market-driven and that to be market-driving companies must not only listen to customers to perceive their needs but also tell customers what the company says they need. "When you're market-driven, one can test and then launch," he explains. "When you're market-driving, one has to adopt the launch-and-learn strategy."

Radical innovators employ a combination of market-driven and market-driving strategies, Kumar says, allocating 5 to 20 percent of their research budgets to radical ideas. It's a risky and potentially expensive strategy. "Instead of learning through research, you learn in the marketplace," says Kumar. "You learn by doing."

As a result, companies escape the incremental innovation that is a product of customer feedback–based product development and rise to the radical innovation characteristic of companies such as Amazon.com, Apple, and Starbucks. Customers don't ask for blockbuster products from these radical innovators, because customers can't envision what doesn't exist. "A few may have imagined the need, perhaps, but not the manifestation of the need."

Kumar asserts that continuous innovation is today's only source of sustainable growth. A company can grow in only two ways: raise prices or increase volume. Not many companies can do the former, he asserts. Achieving the latter means entering new markets—although there is a limit to that as well—and so "the only way to true growth is to develop new products and services through innovation." Make that continuous innovation, because "even the most innovative companies are not about launching . . . and sitting back," Kumar observes. "So innovation is the game in which you have to play continuously." That means you're willing to risk innovation that will sometimes attack your own products.

Cannibals in the Family

Kumar also finds that radical innovators get beyond exclusively incremental innovation through what he calls the three Vs: valued customer, value proposition, and value network. Such concepts, he notes, are far more relevant than product, price, place, and promotion.

The four Ps, he contends, are an essential part of marketing but are inadequate for gaining competitive advantage. Any advantage a company achieves through any of the four Ps is readily open to being matched by competitors. But "by focusing on the three Vs, a company can sustain differentiation."

Having valued customers involves segmenting customers as finely as possible to precisely respond to their perceived value.

Offering a value proposition happens when a company creates the means by which customers perceive its products and services as differentiated from what any competitor offers.

Establishing a value network requires extensive thinking about how a company delivers its value proposition to target customers. "It's a cross-functional orientation often referred to as the value chain," Kumar notes.

"The problem with the four Ps," Kumar believes, "is that they focus toward a more tactical direction in marketing." The three Vs rise to a strategic level and as such are considerably more complex and challenging "because the question becomes where to cut the value network in order to serve the different segments," Kumar says. For each segment, a company theoretically can set up dedicated functions: R&D, marketing, operations, purchasing, distribution, service, and so forth. But that causes the loss of economies of scale.

The challenge lies in segmenting to the exact extent that customers perceive your differentiation from competitors but enough commonality is maintained among the firm's value networks to capture economies of scale.

India Inside

At the Indian Science Conference in 2011, Manmohan Singh, the prime minister of India, sounded a rallying call for Indian scientists: "The time has come for Indian science to once again think big, think out of the box, and think ahead of the times." He heralded a "Decade of Innovation."

All well and good, but as Nirmalya Kumar and Phanish Puranam point out in *India Inside*, for Indians innovation is actually not the great undiscovered land that—largely Western—stereotypes suggest. The stereotype is that Indians don't really do innovation. Bright ideas are bizarrely regarded as a Western preserve. Indians make good accountants and programmers but are not the best at innovation. After all, where are the Indian Googles, iPods, and Viagras?

To refute this common refrain, Kumar and Puranam offer a compelling array of statistics and observations. They point out that Vinod Khosla founded Sun Microsystems, Sabeer Bhatia created Hotmail, Kanwal Rekhi helped develop Ethernet, Narinder Kapany was there at the start of fiber optics, and Vinod Dham was involved in the development of the Pentium chip. All are Indians. Indeed, 26 percent of start-ups in Silicon Valley have an Indian as a founder or a cofounder. Silicon Valley (and the world) owes a considerable and continuing debt to innovative Indians.

Meanwhile, in India daily life offers constant testimony to the innovativeness of Indians. "If you think about innovation more broadly as any novel way of creating value and distributing it, there is a lot of innovation going on in India," says Phanish Puranam.

Also, more formally, India is now home to an array of technological centers for Western multinationals. GE employs 4,300 researchers at its John F. Welch Technology Center in Bangalore. This means that one in six of the technologists who work for GE works at the center. Intel's Xeon 7400 chip, launched in 2008, was designed and developed at its Bangalore center. There are many more examples.

The ramifications of the hidden innovativeness of India are many and are explored in detail by Kumar and Puranam. Over three years, they interviewed managers of multinational companies that have R&D operations in India as well as Indian companies doing R&D in India.

"We realized that the question—Where are the Indian Googles, iPods, and Viagras?—is the wrong question. The right question is: Where is the innovation? Today, in multinational companies, innovation is not done in one location," says Kumar. "The old model of innovation was that R&D was centered usually in the home country or in the lead market, which was another developed country. Innovation today in multinational companies is highly segmented globally. If you look at Apple's iPod, the design was done in America, the manufacturing is done in China, the interface was developed in the United Kingdom, and the software was written in India. So if you ask is it an American invention, yes, it's an American invention, but no new product today is being developed only out of one country. It's a multicountry approach, and multinationals have become very good at setting up these different units across the world, differentiating them to use different pools of expertise, and then integrating them to create a complete product."

This, say Kumar and Puranam, is not a case of "reverse innovation" (the concept created by the Tuck professor Vijay Govindarajan to explain the development of products in emerging markets and then their sale in developed markets—see Chapter 1). "The idea of reverse innovation to us already implies a world that's passed, because it says innovation is innovation only if it ends up in the developed world," says Puranam. "India and China are so large and are going to be so important that companies need to get out of this mentality that if you develop something there, it's worthwhile only if it goes to the rest of the developed world. If it goes to India and China and it remains there, it's big enough and bright enough and profitable enough. If something is big in America, nobody asks, Is it big in the rest of the world?"

Kumar and Puranam contend that what is happening is the rise of globally coordinated distributed R&D processes. This means that no one country can claim that it developed a particular product. (In this they draw a distinction between India and China. In China a lot of the innovation being carried out could be categorized as traditional R&D, which effectively localizes products for the Chinese market.)

The major thrust of *India Inside* is that innovation is practiced in India but for observers who are not inquisitive is largely hidden. Like the chips inside your computer, Indian innovation is quietly and efficiently going about its work, a crucial part of any chain of innovation. Amazon may be regarded as the American online pioneer, but purchases from its website may be processed out of India using software written by Indians on a website in whose development Indians had a hand.

For Kumar, the research behind the book was eye-opening. His book *India's Global Powerhouses* celebrated the rise of a new generation of Indian multinationals but also mourned the lack of Indian innovation. "In *India's Global Powerhouses*, I ended by saying Indian companies are going global, but they need to do innovation. This research revealed to me that there is a lot of innovation happening in India; it's just that I had never seen it or heard about it, because it's invisible."

Emerging Brands Go Global

Brand Breakout, Kumar's 2013 book coauthored with Jan-Benedict Steenkamp, charts the rise of brands from emerging markets as they make the leap from local to global. We talked to Kumar about its major themes at London Business School. As always, it was difficult to break into his fast-talking stream of insights, opinions, facts, and passions.

What was the starting point for this book?

The starting point was really looking at the top companies in the world. If you look, you will see that 25 percent of them are from emerging markets. Look at the richest people in the world and you will find that 25 percent of them are from emerging markets. But look at the top hundred global brands and you will see one from an emerging market: Corona from Mexico. The question is, Why?

When most people in the Western market are asked to name a Chinese brand, they go blank. That's where the idea came from. Then it became not about best practice because nothing exists today but next practice: How would you develop global brands out of emerging markets? That's where we started coming up with the ways people do it.

Related to this is why emerging markets need to develop global brands. This is the whole story that as it becomes more and more expensive for them to produce goods, they're going to have to move forward from simply being the manufacturing capitals of the world.

Another related point is that for almost 40 years China has been a manufacturer for the world. In the next 10 years, the world will manufacture for China. There is no doubt about it.

This transition is taking place. You are starting to see it with respect to luxury goods, the wine market, a lot of the commodity markets, food markets, and oil. China and India are not going to simply be export machines but are also going to become the largest import machines in the world.

That's why you see the Chinese government trying to buy up a lot of businesses and land abroad, whether it's vineyards or dairy farms in New Zealand and Australia or farmland in Africa. In the next 10 to 15 years China will become richer, so they are trying to make sure that the supply will be there.

It sounds as if your research has opened your eyes to the reality of China's emergence.

You could say that. The other learning I had was with respect to the way Chinese companies are put on the stock market. They may own three factories but will put only one factory on the stock market. Alternatively, they might have factories that produce six products and will put one of the products on the stock market.

When you do that, what happens is that you can completely manipulate the results of that one company on the stock market. The factory might be actually running at a loss, or they might have a company that makes juice, makes the juice pulp, makes the juice packaging, makes the juice, and sells it to the market. They will put the bottom end of that juice value chain into the stock market, and then the company has to buy all the juice pulp from the upstream sister company.

There's a whole untold story about the integrity of these companies in terms of stock market listings. Their ownership structures are opaque.

How does Brand Breakout *relate to your previous work?*
Each of my books is a stand-alone book, but this book intersects two things I'm very interested in: emerging markets and marketing. The theme of emerging markets is in there, along with the theme of marketing in India. In the last two books—*India Inside* and *India's Global Powerhouses*—the emphasis was very much on the emergence of India. The three books before that were totally marketing-focused. With this book and the next I'm coming back to the theme of combining emerging markets and marketing.

Why do emerging markets need global brands?
First, they need global brands because basically as the costs go up in emerging markets, they need to go further down the value chain and capture more of the returns; otherwise they're not going to be competitive at some level. So part of it is to get higher levels of profitability. Apple's producer, Hon Hai (also known as Foxconn), makes a 2 percent return on sales; Apple makes a 30 percent return on sales. It's a question of entering more profitable businesses.

Are companies in emerging markets aware of this need?
Yes. In fact, you can pretty much talk to all emerging market countries and all of them recognize the need

to build global brands. We know one thing for sure: no country has ever become developed without having some global brands come out of it. It happened with Korea, it happened with Japan, and it is going to happen with China and other areas. Twenty years ago if I had told you Korea would have global brands, you would have laughed at me. If I told you 40 years ago that Japan would have global brands, you would have laughed at me.

What kind of timelines are you talking about?

With China you can already see that there are brands—such as Lenovo and Haier—that have gone global but may not be top of consumers' minds. In the next decade you will see more, and they will register with consumers: companies such as the Chinese brand Galanz in the microwave industry and Havaianas from Brazil in the sandals industry.

What should companies in the West, in the developed markets, take away from the book?

They are going to find out who their future competitors are. They underestimated the Koreans and the Japanese, so our warning to them is not to underestimate these companies. They are your future competitors, and not only are they your future competitors, some of them are going to buy out some of your best-known companies. Some of these companies are engaged in acquisitions; think of Land Rover and Jaguar, which are now Indian-owned. If they can't build the brand, one of the routes is to acquire brands. It's faster.

Isn't it a very different situation from what happened with Japan and Korea?

It's the same. The differences are in the details, but the big picture is the same. As a country becomes developed, it has more R&D resources, more marketing resources, and the ambition to become global, and so hundreds of them try and maybe 10 will succeed.

It seems that India has a greater awareness of the importance of global brands and is further down the development line than China.

I would say the opposite. I would say in India there are greater branding skills and capabilities, but in the desire to build global brands, China is ahead. Every Chinese manager we talked to spoke about the need to become a global brand. I talked to someone at Shanghai-based Bright Food, and he said, we are constantly thinking, Why can't we be like a Nestlé?

With China there is another difference. Most of the time when developing countries were trying to build global brands in the past, they didn't have quality products. Historically, the Japanese and Koreans didn't have quality products. In China's case, nobody disagrees with the fact that China has world-class manufacturing capabilities. The best products in the world, including the Apple iPhone and the iPad, are made in China.

So they already have the product capability; now they need to add a branding capability. That has got to be easier than the other way around. That is one of our arguments. Let's say there are 1,000 manufacturers in China that have mastered world-class manufacturing. Let's say that out of those 1,000, 100 decide to go build a global brand. Maybe 10 of them will succeed.

Can you see this argument applying elsewhere?
Africa is a bit further behind. In Africa, the only country where we recognize that there might be some emerging global brands is South Africa, because South Africa already has one global brand, which is the restaurant chain Nando's.

Where does this research go next?
My next book is related but different about how global brands from the West need to adapt for emerging markets. We have already interviewed 30 people running global brands. They explain how they're changing their organizational structures to give more importance to emerging markets, how they are changing their product and value propositions to be more in tune with emerging markets, how they're using local brands in emerging markets to develop them for other emerging markets, and how they are acquiring local brands to find the role of a local brand in a global portfolio. It's very interesting.

CHAPTER

8

The Kings of Context

Every idea has its time and place. Most emerge from the maelstrom of the moment, often half formed, in response to events or changing circumstances. The rise of the Indian thinkers and Indian companies profiled in this book is no exception. Their growing influence goes hand in hand with the emergence of India as an economic colossus. As India's status in the world grows, its thinkers have been afforded a growing global audience.

India is suddenly fashionable.

But in truth, even before that country's remarkable resurgence, Indian management thinkers were becoming influential through Western business schools and universities. Yet context is a powerful thing, and the rise of India as a nation means that the ideas of those thinkers have risen on the same tide that has lifted Indian culture and consciousness. Today Indian thinkers are part of the new zeitgeist.

As we have seen in earlier chapters, many of those thinkers made the journey from their homeland to the West decades ago. For many of them that journey had a huge impact on their ideas and left an indelible mark.

This was something we put to Bhaskar Chakravorti when we met him. Chakravorti is senior associate dean, International Business and Finance, and executive director for the Institute for Business in the Global Context at the Fletcher School of Tufts University. Before Fletcher, he was a partner at McKinsey & Company and a distinguished scholar at MIT's Legatum Center for Development and Entrepreneurship. He also served on the faculty of the Harvard Business School and the Harvard University Center for the Environment. He is the author of *The Slow Pace of Fast Change: Bringing Innovations to Market in a Connected World*.

What was the lure of coming to the States?

I studied economics in India at the Delhi School of Economics and was committed to the academic life. After that I came to the United States. I basically wanted to go the best academic department that had expertise in the areas I wanted to work in, which was the field of game theory, and a department that would offer me the largest scholarship because I didn't have a single dollar in my wallet.

One thing led to another. I started off as an academic and went on to do deep research surrounded by people who are exploring all kinds of interesting things ranging from the hidden patterns in graphs and very large numbers to the future of wireless communication and everything else in between. That started sparking a new interest in connecting my intensely theoretical field of specialization, game theory, to a wider universe, and that took me from a quite esoteric, highly mathematical origin to eventually advising the Federal Communications Commission on the idea of using auctions to transfer public radio spectrum to private carriers that would then create this amazing thing called the wireless phone industry.

There was the U.S. government making decisions worth tens of billions of dollars on the basis of what we thought was completely abstract logic.

I went from Bellcore, the part of the old Bell Labs that belonged to the Baby Bells, to Monitor, the most academic of all the consulting firms. The first two and a half years with Monitor I was primarily traveling around Africa trying to develop a fiber optic network that would surround that continent. Through that process and with my work on innovation and long-term global forces later at McKinsey, I learned that some of the hardest innovation and business decisions are made not just on the basis of spreadsheets but on the basis of geopolitics, history, behavioral and cultural anxieties of all kinds.

That got me interested in this whole notion of connecting business logic with what I call contextual intelligence.

How much does your Indian background inform what you're doing now?

Interestingly, I find that it informs it quite a bit for multiple reasons. One is that if you are an immigrant who has moved from one side of the world, both in a physical and a figurative sense, to the other side, you've already developed a certain amount of contextual agility. You recognize that no two cities are the same. Behaviors and choices aren't the same. And at the same time, at their very core, people are the same. Very often we have similar hopes, fears, and dreams, scaled up or down based on different expectations, experiences and contexts. The external environments are very different, and that shapes our behaviors in fundamentally different ways.

I was open to the idea that there is a core of commonality despite the variability in the human condition and all these differences that manifest themselves across different countries, the advanced world, the emerging world, and so on. I think that's one thing that has basically been genetically fixed in me.

The second thing is that growing up in India, you learn to become extremely adaptable to practically everything. India, as it is today and as it has been for centuries, has been constantly bombarded by influences, migrations, conquests, and so on, and India has perennially been a resilient nation. India also prepares you to adapt to many adversities, and you are accustomed to opposite extremes cohabiting spaces right next to each other. Thus, you almost are ready for any eventuality.

It's not that you aren't surprised, but you don't feel overwhelmed, and that has helped me. Being exposed to so many different events and situations made me more of a problem solver with the ability to draw upon multiple people, disciplines, and sources of expertise, which I find enormously valuable.

The third thing that has been helpful is that to some extent Indians have ended up, because of a combination of history and the legacy of the British Empire, being more global citizens than perhaps almost any other nation. You find Indians in all walks of life in practically all parts of the world, doing all kinds of things. There is something about the history of the country and its relationship with the rest of the world that gives us that kind of mobility.

The agility, the adaptability you talk about, is contextual intelligence in your terminology.

Absolutely, because even a passing awareness of India makes one appreciate that there is almost nothing that happens in a linear way in India. There are multiple U-turns and sideways movements. Nonlinearity and randomness are an essential part of how you think about life, and a lot of that actually comes from outside the classic business logic.

A lot of that has to do with politics. It has to do with the state of the human condition. It has to do with the environment. So the context is in the fore-ground, as opposed to being in the background. To my mind contextual knowledge often trumps rational business knowledge because rational business knowledge is easier to appreciate and pick up. It's the contextual knowledge that is much, much harder.

Can the ability to pick up that contextual knowledge be developed?
I believe it can be developed, and it's a combination of exposing people to a variety of experiences and giving them the classical educational experience.

The trouble is that in our graduate institutions we create silos. We send the lawyers off to law school, the businesspeople off to business school, the policy people off to public policy or international affairs schools, and they become separate tribes. Then over the course of their work experiences, they do or do not develop that contextual knowledge. The ones who do develop such knowledge end up becoming the leaders, the innovators, the big-picture thinkers.

But most of the others remain narrow technocrats competent but constrained within their tribal roles. Part of my aspiration is to break down these tribal walls and create a generation of future leaders who are trained to think about issues in an inherently interdisciplinary way.

What you're talking about is a more direct and interactive and topical brand of business education.

That's right. It's taking a problem-solving approach and saying, look, here are some really big, hairy issues, and this requires understanding the problem through tearing it apart by using multiple tools. But it is also necessary to put together solutions, and those solutions themselves require multiple tools.

And contextual intelligence?

Yes, and that largely involves having an awareness of the interconnections between the decisions that you make as a business leader and all the other elements that one normally assumes away, such as, What's the state of the human condition in the part of the world I'm operating in? What's the local and geopolitical situation? What's the level of security, both national security and security in terms of natural resources and human resources? What's the state of the environment in that part of the world? And how do all these elements factor into the business decisions we make?

In business education, we are creating a dangerous precedent in which we oversimplify the kinds of choices managers have to make, and that is resulting in often catastrophic decisions. By this I'm referring not just to what led to the recent financial crisis but also to the Rana Plaza disaster in Bangladesh in 2013. To my mind a lot of that comes directly out of oversimplified frameworks, such as the five forces model that we teach in the first class in strategy in the first year in every business school around the world.

What forms does this oversimplification take?

If you think about the five forces model, it is basically a shorthand way of identifying which parts of the market are the most attractive, and this is done on the basis of where you have an optimum negotiating advantage with other market participants.

When I translate that into negotiating with a Bangladeshi supplier, I optimize my negotiation with that supplier by essentially squeezing the supplier, because I'm a garment retailer or brand and my objectives are to stay competitive in a highly competitive industry. One way in which I do that is to push suppliers as far as I can push them. That's what I'm taught in business to do.

What ends up happening is the suppliers then go back and put their factories in buildings that risk falling down because they want to keep their costs low. As the global supply chain is further and further dispersed into all these parts of the world where the context cannot be taken for granted, where building safety, labor laws, governance structures, legal systems, and environmental laws aren't enforced, we cannot take these things for granted, and that's why there are calamities that are happening not just in Bangladesh.

That's just one example of where I feel that we are preparing people to march off exactly in the wrong direction relative to where we should be going if such global growth is to be sustained. I hope to make a tiny dent, a little detour, from that onward march.

But people don't have much appetite for complexity. When they come to business schools, they want the shorthand and the simplification, don't they?

Absolutely. I've spent time working with managers for almost 20 years, and I think we in academia tend to believe that managers don't have time. Therefore, we need to literally spoon-feed them with pellets of astronaut food. Managers—absolutely true—don't have time, but we don't credit them with the kinds of intelligence they actually have. Managers are on the ground and face the crises that affect them, and they realize that they actually do need a mindset and tools that give them the ability to take an enormous amount of complexity and be able to make good decisions.

Unfortunately, what has happened is that academia is populated by academics who are to a large extent removed from this messy reality, and so we are not serving our ultimate customers very well.

In your current role, what does success look like?

For me, the biggest achievement would be to turn out young men and women who are going to be running institutions 10, 15, 20, maybe even 5 years from now, with this contextual intelligence combined with classic business intelligence, and they will be making wiser decisions. They will be running Gap or H&M and Zara, and they will be doing so in a way in which factory buildings don't have to come down.

They will be managing the next generation of the iPad without having people jump out of factory windows. They will be developing businesses that do not require a drain on natural resources. They will be exploring new markets in places such as sub-Saharan Africa with the awareness that if I'm going to start the next KFC franchise in Kenya, I have to know that there is no poultry supply in eastern Africa or any part of Africa that can actually meet my demand. So I have to figure out not only how to be a best-of-class fried chicken branded retailer but also how to solve the problem in the supply chain and potentially become a technology provider to the nascent poultry industry in that part of the world. My aspiration is to at least give a nudge and provide a framework to help create people who will be able to make those kinds of decisions.

You keep coming back to problem solving.
I keep coming back to problem solving, and for better or for worse, we have lots of big problems to solve.

Thinking 2.0

If context is king, the Indian context has provided inspiration and insight to many others who have been touched by the nation's economic growth and broadening horizons.

Along with the Indian-born thinkers in this book, we have included one or two thinkers from neighboring territories whose ideas were forged in the same intellectual furnace. Subir Chowdhury, for example, was born in Bangladesh and went to the Indian Institute of Technology at Kharagpur.

It is also clear that there is a cadre of second-generation Indian thinkers with a distinctively Indian perspective. Although they were born outside India, the influence of their parents and their exposure to Indian culture and ways of thinking mean that they bring a different perspective to the cultures in which they grew up. East meets West in a potent cultural cauldron. Many of these thinkers combine Indian-sounding names with American or English accents. In this regard, they are like other first-generation immigrants, straddling two worlds, open to the opportunities of both, and hostage to the traditions of neither.

The second-generation thinkers include people such as Sheena Iyengar, Deepa Prahalad, and Rakesh Khurana.

Born in Toronto, Canada, after her parents emigrated there from Delhi, Sheena Iyengar is the S.T. Lee Professor of Business at Columbia Business School, where she has taught since 1998. Her bestselling 2010 book *The Art of Choosing,* a fascinating investigation into how we make choices in everyday life, was short-listed for the Financial Times and Goldman Sachs Business Book of the Year Award in 2010.

Iyengar was named a member of the Thinkers50 in 2011. Her parents moved to Flushing, Queens, in 1972, where her father helped establish the first permanent Sikh temple, and in 1979 the family moved to New Jersey. Iyengar grew up in a bicultural environment, observing the tenets of Sikhism with her family but participating in American culture outside her home.

She explained her fascination with choice in an interview with Big Think.com:

I think I was always informally thinking about choice from when I was a very young child because I was born to Sikh immigrant parents, so I was constantly going back and forth between a Sikh household and an American outside world, so I was going back and forth between a very traditional Sikh home in which you had to follow the Five Ks. You know never cut your hair, always carry around a comb, never take off your underwear even if it was in the shower, dress very conservatively, and so on. I was living, growing up in a very traditional household and yet at the same time I was going to school in the United States where I was taught the importance of personal preference.

So at home it was all about learning your duties and responsibilities, whereas in school it was all about, well, you get to decide what you want to eat. You get to decide how you're going to look and what you're going to be when you grow up, and when people learned that my parents actually had an arranged marriage, people thought that was the most horrific thing on earth. I mean how could anybody allow their marriage of all things to be prescribed by somebody else? And you know I went home and my parents seemed normal. They didn't seem to feel like somehow they had been victims of some Nazi camp or something. So it was constantly going back and forth between these two cultures that kept raising the question, well, how important is personal freedom? And I think that has always been of interest to me.

Then, the other thing that affected my interest in choices growing up was the fact that I was going blind [Iyengar was diagnosed at an early age with a rare form of retinitis pigmentosa and was fully blind by the time she reached high school, able to perceive only light] and that meant that there were lots of questions that constantly kept arising about how much choices I actually could have.*

Deepa Prahalad, the daughter of C. K. Prahalad, is a business strategist and management thinker in her own right. In *Predictable Magic (*2011), coauthored with the industrial designer Ravi Sawhney, she examines why whereas 80 percent of new products fail or underperform, a few rare products exceed expectations. Why is this? Because, she says, their creators don't focus on delivering utilitarian objects; instead, they craft rewarding experiences that have emotional resonance for their users.

Prahalad and Sawhney introduce the idea of *Psycho-Aesthetics*, a way of creating deep emotional connections between consumers and brands that can be transferred to new products. The ability to develop Psycho-Aesthetics enables companies to unleash the power of design strategy to create the predictable magic of the book's title.

Rakesh Khurana is probably the best known of the second-generation Indian thinkers. He has been included in the Thinkers50 ranking since 2007. Khurana is the Marvin Bower Professor of Leadership at Harvard Business School. He is best known for his books *Searching for a Corporate Savior: The Irrational Quest for Charismatic CEOs* (2002) and *From Higher Aims to Hired Hands: The Social Transformation of American Business Schools and the Unfulfilled Promise of Management as a Profession* (2007).

---

* http://bigthink.com/users/sheenaiyengar.

In the latter book, Khurana argues that business schools set out with the grand idea of professionalizing management. However, that remains an unfinished project. "My argument is that in addition to questions about the efficacy of the degree, most MBAs want their work to have meaning; they want to be professionals. But business schools are not providing some way for them to link their personal values to the work they are going to be doing."

Khurana is one of Harvard's rising stars. His criticism is measured and is the more damning for it. His book is an impressive tour of the social and intellectual history of American university business schools. It reveals how the desire to raise management first to a profession and later to a science has driven business education and shaped American management for more than a century.

The origins of U.S. B-schools lie in the late nineteenth century, he argues, when members of an emerging managerial elite, seeking social status to match the wealth and power they had acquired, began working with major universities. The new commercial barons set out to establish graduate business education programs paralleling those for medicine and law.

In their attempt to make management a profession, they faced serious hurdles. They needed to codify knowledge that was relevant for management practitioners and develop enforceable standards of conduct. That was not easy.

Drawing on a rich set of archival material from business schools, foundations, and academic associations, Khurana traces how the fledgling U.S. B-schools confronted those challenges with varying strategies during the Progressive era and the Depression, the postwar boom years, and the recent decades of freewheeling capitalism.

But the book is more than just a historical odyssey; it is also a heartfelt plea for business schools to rediscover their higher purpose.

The university-based business schools, including Harvard, where Khurana is employed, were founded to train a professional class of managers akin to doctors and lawyers. But, he argues forcefully, they have retreated from that goal. That has left a moral vacuum at the center of business education and, arguably, management itself.

In recent years, Khurana argues, business schools have largely capitulated in the battle for professionalism and have become mere purveyors of a product, the MBA. The professional and moral ideals that once inspired their teaching have been eclipsed by a view that the only significant measure of managers is their ability to create shareholder value.

Ultimately, though, this is an abdication of responsibility. Khurana believes the time has come to upgrade the training of our future business leaders and complete the professionalization project.

When we spoke to Khurana, he explained the importance of his Indian heritage.

> I was born in India. I came to the United States when I was nearly four. I am a second-generation immigrant.
>
> There's much more diversity in academia now than 25 years ago, not just Indians but women and people of color.
>
> As a consequence of the changing economics of India as a software-developing nation and a greater

focus on China and on globalization, there's a much greater sensitivity and sense that the centers of the economic future may be more than simply the traditional Western European and North American nexus. We are seeing a dramatic shift as India arises in the service sector with a highly educated workforce and a historically entrepreneurial society, coupled with China's rise as a major power.

As the number of Indians has increased among immigrant populations, the second generation of Indians tend to be less self-conscious about participating in larger societal debates. You see that in literature in particular, with the wider consciousness of Indian and Chinese literature. This kind of second generation of identity contributes to a wider consciousness of the culture. This is not new. We saw it in the United States with the Irish immigrant influence in the nineteenth century and the Jewish immigrants in the twentieth century.

Any immigrant definitely feels a dual sense of identity: you have an outsider's perspective on every institution. For me personally, the contrast between Eastern and Western philosophy tended to be fairly wide. The assumptions that my parents had about society and your responsibilities to your family and even the importance of professions were very different from those I encountered where I was growing up. That tension or dialectic often means you feel like an "other" in both groups—not completely Indian with your family and not completely American either.

Where is your thinking influenced by your Indian background?

There is one area where it deeply influences my perspective. That is the importance of duty and service in life. There's a very strong orientation toward the idea that one doesn't get fulfilment through individualism but rather that fulfillment and duty in life really involve advancing the community, and that means the collective family, the collective town you live in. Ultimately that becomes how one gains fulfillment and how one performs one's duty. I find this is the sort of questioning that guides me: What is my obligation to my students? What is my obligation to my research and to society? That definitely colors a lot of my general mindset.

Anyone who comes from a communitarian society probably feels that. My parents amplified that being in America, they swung the pendulum even further in that direction, so maybe I got a slightly artificial version of those values growing up in New York City compared with what I would have had growing up in India. I had to take my parents' word for it.

Playing Catch-Up

There is also a feeling that researchers are now beginning to make useful sense of what has happened in India and what is happening in today's Indian organizations. When economic explosions happen, theory has a nasty habit of lagging helplessly behind. Now, slightly breathless, it is catching up, beginning to make sense of best Indian practice and the useful lessons.

The next generation of Indian thinkers is already hard at work. They include Kamalini Ramdas and Rajesh Chandy at London Business School, Anindya Ghose and Arun Sundararajan at New York University's Stern School of Business, Ravi Bapna of the Carlson School of the University of Minnesota, and Vallabh Sambamurthy of Michigan State. There are many others.

Among the upcoming Indian-born thinkers is Kiron Ravindran of IE Business School. His work is practically focused and illustrates the trend of thinkers turning their research to deal with issues that have been produced by India's emergence.

We talked with Kiron Ravindran in his office in Madrid.

What is the guiding force behind your work?
It started out when I did a PhD to basically understand why outsourcing projects were going wrong. We figured there was something deeper than not speaking the right dialect, having an accent problem, or miscommunication. I wanted to make a difference to the kind of job I was exposed to, as mad as that sounds!

Tell us about the devil's triangle.
The term goes back to the early days of IT consulting. The devil's triangle is that problems arise from clients who don't know what they want or ask meaningless questions, vendors who comply with those meaningless things or are trying to push their own software, and system integrators who are trying to make money in

the middle by pushing more IT than is required, convincing clients they need more than they really need.

Where is your research now focused?

At the end of my PhD I became wiser and realized there is no single clear solution to why IT outsourcing often encounters problems. Instead, there are various elements that might contribute to success or failure. Then I started getting interested in sociological theories that argued that how connected you are to people can affect your relationships and the success of whatever interaction you're involved in. I tried to apply this in the context of companies. They don't operate in a vacuum but instead always operate embedded in a network of other companies, so is there a way to find out if you can predict success or failure based on how connected companies are by themselves?

Perhaps companies that are more embedded in a network of other companies do better. In the same way that people with higher reputations are more likely to behave well because the stakes are higher, companies with the higher reputational capital are probably more likely to stick to their contracts because the stakes are higher. If they deviate from the contract, more people will know about it.

Thus, in outsourcing, if a company has many contracts with other people or other companies, that company is probably going to behave well.

There is this one predictor, which I call social capital, that is based on the number of contracts or who you're connected with and so on and is an indicator of how trustworthy or how reliable a company is. This means a client could evaluate a vendor or a vendor could evaluate a client by looking at who they're connected to and then deciding to award a longer or a shorter contract; therefore, this reputational capital translates to economic value in terms of a longer contract.

When you go to talk to companies and executives in companies, do they understand the value of social capital?

They get the general idea. Who you're friends with says something about you. That's intuitive.

The difficult part is, How do I measure it, or how do I go about putting this in practice? Can I convert this one additional friend to an extra month of a contract? That is the difficult part to convince people about, but statistically my data cover some 20,000 contracts over the last 20 years.

Are there different cultural attitudes within this?

There are actually a lot of indicators that this would be strongly influenced by culture. There are very interesting studies on how governments or people hold other people accountable in countries that have poor legal systems. In Vietnam, for instance, if you deviate once from the social norms, you're ostracized from the marketplace.

Nobody deviates because it's communal enforcement; it's far more powerful than any legal measure of enforcement. I think to some extent that's what happens in large IT outsourcing, because it's difficult to enforce these things in the code of law. It's complicated, it takes a lot of time and money, and so the fear that you will be ostracized by this community and not get another contract is probably a strong driver of good behavior. If this taboo holds in the industry, it's likely that in more collective cultures you would find a strong binding to this social capital–based behavior.

Which companies understand this? Where is the best practice?

The traditional Big Six have been doing this fairly well for a while now. IBM, HP, EDF, which is now part of HP, have been doing this fairly well historically, but I think we are seeing emerging companies, especially Indian companies such as MForce and Tata, that are getting high-value long-term projects and, possibly as a result of consistently winning these signature, high-caliber projects, contracts. I think that's paying off for them, and I'm guessing that over time, we'll see them competing more and more with the IBMs of the world not just on cost but in terms of quality and competence and innovation and things like that.

You've watched the rise of India economically from various perspectives. You were in California, and now you're in Madrid. It must be a strange experience watching your own country being transformed and, more interestingly, people's perceptions of India and of Indian companies being transformed.

That's right. I entered my undergraduate course in 1991, the year India deregulated, so everybody who entered engineering school in my year went in with unbelievable optimism, because we knew that the markets had opened up. We came out in 1995, and there were so many more opportunities. We would get jobs fresh out of campus, and that carried on past the dot-com boom. That was when morale dropped a bit, but I think what came out in this process is that we were shaken out of complacently thinking that things would continue just the way they were.

Suddenly the idea that you could make a difference crept in. Until then, you worked in the job you got and retired in that job. You basically tried as hard as you could to maintain job security. But by 2000, people would leave jobs on a whim just because they could, just because there were other jobs available, just because the market looked positive, and I think that's had a longer-term impact. It changed the way people thought about their contributions to their careers and their lives and what they could do by themselves.

Are you optimistic about what's happening in India?

In the long term, I'm very optimistic about India for multiple reasons. One is that we've got a few really good people managing a few really good companies, and the difference is going to be very obvious very soon if it is not already.

Look at the universal identity (UID) project, which is basically trying to give an identity number and an identity card to 1 billion people. There is no other country in the world that has attempted something on this scale, and it's being led by a manager from an IT company. Of course, he's the founder of the IT company, but it's still an IT guy leading this project, and that is impressive. We're not just doing Java code for a company in Silicon Valley anymore.

What can and should Western leaders learn from India, do you think? What are they missing when they look at India and the way Indian companies are managed and led? You've talked about comfort with ambiguity, but is there something else that Western companies don't understand or miss?

It really is a question of the balance of yin and yang. There are always multiple rights. There's always a different perspective. There's always a different legacy that the other person is carrying with him or her that if you understand, you understand why this person behaves the way he or she does. It was Bertrand Russell who said that everything you hear about India is true and the opposite is also true.

When Satya Nadella was appointed CEO of Microsoft, the blogs were wondering, now, what's the big change he's going to do, and he said he's going to make no big change. And if you've come from the Jack Welch school of thought, how can you be the new CEO, the turnaround guy, and not make any big changes?

But I think that's the embodiment of good, new management, to say, okay, you don't necessarily need to make change for the sake of making change. Let's figure out why these things are working the way they are and then make the small changes that we need. If you can work with the current constraints, you can make the change you need to make.

CHAPTER
9

Thinking at Work

There is nothing as practical as a great idea, and so we would like to finish by recounting the stories of some of the most impressive business leaders and organizations we have encountered. Their stories are testimony to the power of many of the ideas we have discussed.

A while ago we wrote an article about the Indian company Infosys. It brought home to us how different the Indian take on corporate and commercial reality is.

Infosys is an Indian business legend—justifiably. Its story is so fantastic that if it had happened in Silicon Valley, it would be a movie. The story of the $250 loan to Narayana Murthy in 1981 bears repetition. The loan came from his wife. The IT engineer set up the company in Pune with six other engineers. It reached annual revenues of $100 million in 1999, $200 million in 2000, $400 million in 2001, $500 million in 2002, $1 billion in 2004, $3 billion in 2007, and $5 billion in 2010. Now the first Indian company to be listed on the Nasdaq has 150,000 employees, a market value of $32 billion, and annual sales of $7 billion.

To those uninitiated in the ways of the company colloquially known an Infy, this feels like an archetypal dreams-to-reality Indian story. It isn't. Indeed, Infosys exemplifies many of the outstanding characteristics of the best Indian management.

Infosys's first stroke of genius was one of optimism or bold ambition, depending on one's perspective. It began life with a global view. The world was its market from the very start. India's domestic market had little attraction for the simple reason that in the early 1980s there weren't enough Indian corporations to buy the services Infosys offered.

"Posterity will not excuse you if you did not dream big," says Narayana Murthy. "You owe it to your customers, your colleagues, your investors, and society. Every major civilization, every great advance in science and technology, and every great company are built on a big dream."

The vision of Infosys remains the same as it was from day 1: "We will be a globally respected corporation." It has a compelling simplicity, a built-in narrative that makes the company's success appear all but inevitable. (Perhaps the most obvious comparison is that of Thomas Watson Sr., renaming the Computing Tabulating and Recording Company as International Business Machines when it didn't have a customer outside the United States.)

The Infosys way has been examined from an array of angles. Its management of people has been justly celebrated, as has its commitment to ethical business and its global aspirations and character. Its mission is "To achieve our objectives in an environment of fairness, honesty, and courtesy toward our clients, employees, vendors, and society at large," and its stated values are "We believe that the softest pillow is a clear conscience."

"The factors that differentiate a corporation from its competitors are an enduring value system, open-mindedness, a pluralistic and meritocratic approach, and practicing speed, imagination, and excellence in execution. Leaders have to focus on creating such an environment," Narayana Murthy has observed.

In talking to Infosys executives, two other things are eye-catching. First, there is an air of thoughtfulness to the company and its people. You would expect that in such a fast-growing company there would be a derring-do air of opportunism. Instead, the company's leaders are actively cerebral rather than blindly active.

"If you look at the motto of the company and our business cards, it says 'powered by intellect and driven by values.' Both of those lines are extremely serious for the company because we really think hard about what we are doing and why. You can do all the training and all the good stuff, but when you hit the field and the gunshot is fired, you run like hell," quipped Senior Vice President Sanjay Purohit when we spoke.

Second, despite its headline-grabbing growth, Infosys manages to juggle the short term and the long term adroitly. Its leaders appear skilled in zooming in to tackle the nitty-gritty of delivering complex projects and zooming out to look at the broader picture.

"If you're really serious about client value, then it's not only about short-term value, it's about long-term value; you have to understand where the clients' value would come from over time and how we are prepared," says Purohit, who joined the company in 2000. "I am not working for a company per se. I'm not in a job; I'm actually building something which is of value to our clients, it's of value to our employees, it's of value to our shareholders. Way back in 2000, perhaps 2001, I stopped working *for* Infosys and I started working *with* Infosys."

Other employees echoed these comments. One told us that he treated Infosys with the respect and care he would show if it were his own company. This refrain is commonplace among Infoscions. Whereas other companies would be destabilized by fast growth and quickly lose touch with their foundations, Infoscions are engaged. This is not by chance.

Infosys was the first Indian company to offer stock options to employees. Its commitment to training and development is similarly distinctive. Much of this takes place at a 337-acre campus in Mysore, the biggest corporate training facility in the world, described by one commentator as "the Taj Mahal of training centers."

It is also connected with the best academic institutions. Infosys works with more than 105 colleges across the world. It handpicks the institutions drawn from different streams, such as management, technology, and liberal arts.

This means that interns to the company are not hired on the virtually random basis adopted by other companies. Instead, they are carefully selected and nurtured. Says Sanjay Purohit: "The best leaders of tomorrow will come out of these colleges, so we are not going to take a short-term view, which is what most companies do. We want to ensure that we build relationships with some-body who will become a CEO, COO, CFO, or CIO tomorrow. We would like them to understand and appreciate the work we are trying to do because tomorrow when they get into leadership positions, they will understand our emphasis and take their decisions more intelligently."

Employees First

Of course, Infosys is only one Indian success story. Many others are worthy of attention and emulation. Consider HCL Technologies. HCL has cut a defiant swath through management orthodoxy, proclaiming that employees rather than customers should come first.

Its philosophy is distilled down to two words: *Employees First*, "a unique management approach that unshackles the creative energies of our 85,335-plus employees and puts this collective force to work in the service of customers' business problems."

In practice, this means that there is an emphasis on transparency. HCL rates managers on aspects of their performance that include strategic vision, ability to communicate, problem-solving skills, and responsiveness. There is nothing unusual in running such a process. What is unusual is that the results of the survey—the numbers and the comments—are aggregated and published online for every employee to look at.

It may be soft, but HCL is highly successful. Hard performance figures validate its softly, softly approach. Indeed, HCL has numbers aplenty to back up its humanity. Its 2012 results saw revenue reach $4.1 billion, up more than 17 percent; there was a fivefold increase in $100 million–plus clients; and during the year, Eli Lilly, a global pharmaceutical corporation and HCL opened a Co-Innovation Lab in Singapore for developing novel technologies.

Among more than 3,000 technology companies in the Bloomberg database, there are only 7 with revenue of more than $2.5 billion, a market capitalization of more than $5 billion, and a compounded annual growth rate greater than 25 percent during the last five years. HCL Technologies is one of those seven.

The Art of Rafting

Stopping off at HCL's London office—one of HCL's 31 world-wide—to learn about the hard facts and hard work that lie behind the soft stuff, we met the then company CEO and vice chairman, Vineet Nayar. Nayar, the author of a bestselling book on the HCL way (*Employees First, Customers Second*), is bearishly affable. "Six hundred percent growth in seven years; what else can you ask for?" he observes with a smile. "Employees first gave us a competitive advantage."

Vineet Nayar joined HCL in 1985 as a management trainee and worked his way up through the company, becoming president of HCL Technologies (there is also a sister company, HCL Infosystems) in 2005.

Growth brings its own problems. Headlong growth brings expectations, at the very least. Nayar has little truck with the concept of growth providing problems. "If you start seeing challenges as challenges and not as opportunities, then you should not be in management. If you're a Formula 1 racing car driver, do you see bends as opportunities or do you see bends as threats?

"The history of HCL is a bet on the growth of technology services. Back in the late 1990s, 45 percent of our revenues came from technology development. We were very good at what we did. But when the technology meltdown happened in 2000, technology spending vanished overnight, so we had to reinvent our business model. We took a look at our market space, and the key trend was that there was too much emphasis on volume and people had forgotten the concept of value. Everybody was rushing to India, but no one was asking, 'Am I getting value?' I believed that down the line clients would get frustrated: 'I have got my 30 percent, 40 percent cost saving; now what?'"

HCL decided to position itself as a value-centric company rather than a volume-centric company. "We decided to chase deals where we were both important to the customers and creating value for them," Nayar explains.

Nayar believes that the global slowdown that started in 2008 has played straight into HCL's responsive hands. "So you are the team that rows in still waters better than anybody else. That's fine. Now suddenly there's turbulence, and you need to do river rafting. Most companies keep crying that the environment is not good for rowing—our rowing skills are not being used, and we're waiting for the environment to settle down so we can row again. No. Managers cannot be married to what they are good at. They have to be good at what the environment seeks from them. Otherwise they should step out of the way and let somebody else do what is required. This is a time to river raft, to start intuitively driving the boat, and there is an opportunity. At HCL we need to become the best river rafter in town."

Innovating Innovation

Vineet Nayar argues that the way we approach innovation needs reevaluating, reenergizing, and rethinking. "If innovation is created inside the organization, it is measured in the same way it measures everything else," he notes. "Innovation needs to be taken out of the organization and incubated. It needs to be more intuitive. Innovations are often stumbled upon, and that requires openness."

Nayar is currently working on experiments in which employees can work a day for a social cause while being paid by the company. The only conditions are that they must do so in teams of 30 and the youngest person must be the CEO. A total of 37,000 employees from HCL have become involved.

For Nayar, faith-based organizations remain an inspiration. He envies their unifying sense of purpose. "Employees First energized the corporation. It made management accountable," he says. "But today is what matters. Here and now. The human mind is not built for the past. The whole legacy thing is crap." Belief is everything. Belief can change the world.

An Entrepreneurial End

As we were finalizing the manuscript for this book, we talked with the Indian entrepreneur Ronnie Screwvala, who has cut a colorful and hugely successful swath through the media world over the last 30 years, from Bollywood to Disney.

Screwvala launched India's first cable network in 1981. In the 1990s, he went onto create UTV. Today it is one of India's largest media and entertainment conglomerates, spanning motion pictures, broadcasting, television, games, and digital. In 2005, Screwvala took UTV public with a market capitalization of $55 million, and seven years later the Walt Disney Company bought UTV at an enterprise value of $1.4 billion.

At school, Screwvala told us, he had been involved in the theater and then did a lot of front-of-camera hosting. His theatrical career reputedly came to an end when he chose to spend time on his own toothbrush business rather than attend rehearsals.

The crossroads for Screwvala came after he graduated and was thinking about what to do next. His father, as fathers do, advocated steadiness and safety in the form of accountancy. Screwvala wanted to become an entrepreneur but acquiesced and took a job. He lasted three months.

"Very early on I realized it is not in my DNA to implement somebody else's vision, though at that stage I would not have been able to articulate it," says Screwvala. "You need to understand that in India, being an entrepreneur was—and is—not the easiest thing. Twenty years ago most people thought you became an entrepreneur only if you couldn't get a good job anywhere else. It was almost nonaspirational, and the ecosystem from friends and family onward is not supportive."

He created his first media business in 1981 and went on to form UTV, which is involved in broadcasting, gaming, film, and other businesses. He has been involved in a huge number of hit movies as a producer or coproducer, from *Dil Ke Jharoke Main* to *Chennai Express* via *Husbands in Goa* and *Hook Ya Crook*. Along the way, he also launched India's most popular children's channel, Hungama.

"As you sort of get into entrepreneurship, you realize that failure is not actually a full stop. In many ways it's a comma because if you treat it as a full stop, then you might as well pack up. If you consider it a comma, then there is always something that you need to write after that," Screwvala told us. "You can define failure as a mistake, you can define failure as a setback, you can define failure as a speed bump, or sometimes it gets even worse and you end up broke. But that's only the end of the road at that particular moment in that particular situation, segment, or business.

"People say the ratio for successful entrepreneurs is 1 in 10, sometimes 1 in 20 or 30. That kind of bewilders me a little. I understand the uncertainly, but it's just that they have decided not to stay that particular course. If you decide that you're going to stay the course, you have to meander. You are still an entrepreneur. I think one of the key factors in my success is my tenacity, my willingness to stay the course."

Much the same could be said of India. Failure is not an option; it must only be a comma. The rest of the Indian story is being written by those with ideas and the ability to make them work.

Acknowledgments

We would like to thank all the Indian thinkers featured in this book and those we have interviewed over the years.

In particular, thanks are due to Bhaskar Chakravorti, Ram Charan, Subir Chowdhury, Pankaj Ghemawat, Vijay Govindarajan, Anil K. Gupta, Nirmalya Kumar, Vineet Nayar, Navi Radjou, and Kiron Ravindran.

We would like to pay special tribute to two hugely influential thinkers: Sumantra Ghoshal and C. K. Prahalad. We were lucky enough to meet both Sumantra and C.K. on a number of occasions. Both died when they were at the peak of their intellectual powers. Their ideas have proved powerfully prescient in India and far beyond and have had an enormous impact on our lives as well as those of many others.

Index

action-taking ability, 22
Africa, and global brands, 132
Ahuja, Simone, 88
ambiguity, 10–11
Apple, 129
apps, 91
The Art of Choosing (Iyengar), 143
aspiration, 12

Bapna, Ravi, 150
Bartlett, Chris, 4, 15–16
Bhangra music, 7
Bhatia, Sabeer, 124
Bias for Action (Ghoshal and Bruch), 17
BOP. *See* bottom of the pyramid (BOP)
Bossidy, Larry, 4

bottom of the pyramid (BOP), 39, 46–48
See also The Fortune at the Bottom of the Pyramid (Prahalad)
Brand Breakout (Kumar and Steenkamp), 126–132
Breakthrough Idea Award, 48, 74
bricolage, 86
See also jugaad innovation
Bruch, Heike, 17
business schools, 58–59, 145–147

Canada, 100
capitalism
    ethical and societal
        obligations of, 4–5

capitalism (*continued*)
  new ideas of, 43–44
  See also shareholder
      capitalism
CellScope, 91
centrality of the individual,
      33–34
CEOs
  essential attributes for, 57
  failures, 58–59
  successions, 57–58
Chakravorti, Bhaskar, 134–142
Chandler, Alfred, 111
Chandy, Rajesh, 149
Charan, Ram, 2, 4, 52–60
China, 112–114, 128
  and global brands, 131–132
Chowdhry, Bhagwan, 46–47
Chowdhury, Subir, 60–72,
      142
Cinnamon Club, 49–52
C. K. Prahalad Breakthrough
      Idea Award, 48
co-creation, 30–33, 38, 41–42,
      44
commodities, 103
companies, as most important
      institutions of modern
      society, 24–25
Competing for the Future
      (Prahalad and Hamel), 28
connectivity, 42–43
context, India's rise, 133–134
contextual intelligence, 135,
      137–139
core competencies, 28, 41
corporate philosophy, 18
corruption, 63–64
creative capitalism, 43–44
culture, 56

Deming, W. Edwards, 1
democratization of commerce,
      41–43
devil's triangle, 150
Dham, Vinod, 124
DIY, 85, 90
  See also jugaad innovation

economics of quality, 65–69
emerging economies, jugaad
      innovation in, 89–90
emerging markets, and
      marketing, 129–130
emotional capital, 22
enrichment, 71–72
entrepreneurship, 165–166
eurozone, 106
execution, 56–57
Execution (Charan, Bossidy
      and Burck), 4, 56–57

failure, of CEOs, 58–59
fair markets, 44
Feldstein, Martin, 99
Financial Access @ Birth (FAB),
      46–47
financial capital, 18–19
Ford, 93–94
*The Fortune at the Bottom of the
      Pyramid* (Prahalad), 5,
      28–29, 37–39
four Ps, 122, 123
Foxconn, 129
Friedman, Thomas, 98, 99
From Higher Aims to Hired Hands
      (Khurana), 145–147
frugal innovation, 95–96
The Future of Competition
      (Prahalad and
      Ramaswamy), 5, 28

GE. *See* General Electric
General Electric, 74, 124
  bottlenecks in organizational
    culture, 78–79
  and globalization, 107–108
  Jeff Immelt's legacy, 80–81
  and reverse innovation,
    76–77
Gerstner, Lou, 58
Getting China and India Right
    (Gupta and Wang), 112
Ghandi, Mohandas (Mahatma),
    36, 45
Ghemawat, Pankaj, 9, 98–108
Ghose, Anindya, 149–150
Ghoshal, Sumantra, 2, 4, 8
  on holistic view of
    management and
    leadership, 10
  legacy of, 15–25
  on shareholder capitalism,
    9
global brands, 131–132
global capabilities, 12
global firms, 16
global megatrends, 113
global mindset, creating within
    organizations, 79–80
globalization, 8–9, 24–25,
    98–108
  companies' response to,
    107–108
  reversing, 106–107
glocalization, 75–76, 78
Google, as a co-creator, 31
Govindarajan, Vijay "VG", 2–3,
    8, 73–83, 111
  on globalization, 9
Gupta, Anil K., 27–28,
    109–115

HCL Technologies, 161–164
historical success as a bottleneck,
    78–79
Hon Hai, 129
Huawei, 112
human capital, 19, 20, 21–22

IBM, 89–90
The Ice Cream Maker
    (Chowdhury), 60
Immelt, Jeff, 74, 79
  legacy of at General Electric,
    80–81
India, and China, 112–114
India Inc., 117
  rise of, 118–119
India Inside (Kumar and
    Puranam), 123–124,
    126
Indian innovation, 123–126
Indian school of management,
    4–6
Indian thinkers, 1–3
  next generation, 149–156
  reasons for rise in influence
    of, 3–4
  second-generation, 142–149
India's Global Powerhouses
    (Kumar), 126
India's rise, 11–13, 114–115,
    153–155
  context, 133–134
The Individualized Corporation
    (Ghoshal and Bartlett), 17
information architecture, 38
Infosys, 157–161
innovation, 122, 163–164
  frugal innovation, 95–96
  in India, 123–126
  jugaad innovation, 83–96

innovation (*continued*)
in multinational companies, 125
reverse innovation, 74, 75, 76–77, 125
interdependence of institutions, 34
international firms, 16
international integration, 102–103
Iyengar, Sheena, 143–145

jugaad innovation, 83–96

Kant, Ravi, 5–6
Kapany, Narinder, 124
Khosla, Vinod, 124
Khurana, Rakesh, 6–7, 145–149
on globalization, 9
on management as a profession, 10
KISS, 91–92
Kumar, Nirmalya, 3
on ambiguity, 11
on India Inc., 118–119
launch-and-learn strategy, 121–122
marketing, 119–121

launch-and-learn strategy, 121–122
leaders
characteristics of in the new era, 44–45
failures, 58–59
leadership, 35–36
and jugaad innovation, 93–94
role models, 59

Lévi-Strauss, Claude, 86
listening, 71
Lorsch, Jay, 111

Mahajan, Vijay, 46
Mahindra, 112–113
Maker Movement, 86, 90
See also jugaad innovation
management, as a profession, 10, 145–147
management philosophy, 18–19
Managing Across Borders (Ghoshal and Bartlett), 4, 15–16
market-driving vs. market-driven, 121–122
marketing, 119–121
and emerging markets, 129–130
four Ps, 122, 123
three Vs, 122, 123
microconsumers, 42
moral authority, 36, 45
multilateral coordination, 105–106
multinational corporations, forms of, 15–17
multinational/multidomestic firms, 16
Murthy, Narayana, 157–158, 159

N = 1, 31, 34
Nadella, Satya, 117, 155
Naipaul, V.S., 7
Nano car, 86
Nayar, Vineet, 162–164
The New Age of Innovation (Prahalad), 29
new business realities, 17–18

new technologies, 40
Nohria, Nitin, 2, 10

optimization, 72

partnering, 93
Pascale, Richard, 1
Peters, Susan, 81
Piramal, Gita, 2
political freedom, 41
Porter, Michael, 111
The Power of LEO (Chowdhury),
       60
Prabhu, Jaideep, 87–88
Prahalad, C. K., 1, 4, 8
    academics and practitioners,
         27–28
    bio, 28
    co-creation, 30–33
    early life, 29–30
    *The Fortune at the Bottom of
         the Pyramid*, 4–5
    The Future of Competition, 5
    on India's rise, 11–13
    publications, 28–29
Prahalad, Deepa, 145
Predictable Magic (Prahalad and
       Sawhney), 145
process quality, 61–63
professor in residence, 74,
       81–82
protectionism, 102–103
Psycho-Aesthetics, 145
Puranam, Phanish, 123–124
Purohit, Sanjay, 159–161
purpose, process, people
       philosophy, 19
pyramid
    bottom of the pyramid
         (BOP), 39

straddling the, 37–38
    *See also The Fortune at the
         Bottom of the Pyramid*
         (Prahalad)

quality, 61–63
    applying at a national level,
         65
    and corruption, 63–64
    economics of, 65–69
*The Quest for Global
       Dominance* (Gupta and
       Govindarajan), 111

R = G, 31, 34
Radjou, Navi, 83–96
Ramdas, Kamalini, 149
rare earths, 103
Ravindran, Kiron, 150–156
    on ambiguity, 10–11
reach, 120
regulation, 102–103, 105–106
Rekhi, Kanwal, 124
reverse innovation, 74, 75,
       76–77, 125
rooted cosmopolitans, 104
Roy, Arundhati, 7
Roy, Jamini, 119
Russell, Bertrand, 155

Salesforce.com, 92
Sambamurthy, Vallabh, 150
Sawhney, Ravi, 145
Scott, Lee, 107
Screwvala, Ronnie, 164–166
semiglobalization, 100
    See also globalization
Sen, Amartya, 2
shareholder capitalism, 9, 19–20
shareholders, 20

Silicon Valley, cloning, 113–114
The Silk Road Rediscovered
        (Gupta and Wang), 112
Singh, Vivek, 49–52
Sloan, Alfred, 18
social architecture, 38
social capital, 21–22, 151–152
    and cultural attitudes,
        152–153
social fabric, quality of, 23
speed, 120
Steenkamp, Jan-Benedict, 126
succession planning, 57–58
Sundararajan, Arun, 149–150
sustainability, 45–46
synthesizing, 6–7

Tagore, Rabindranath, 119
talent, 23
Tata, Jamsetji Nusserwanji, 5
Tata, Ratan, 5
Tata Group, 5
Tata Nano, 40–41
Taylor, Frederick, 1
TechShop, 93–94
textile production, 68–69
three Vs, 122, 123

tire industry, 32–33
Total Quality Management, 60
transnational firms, 16–17
transparency, 44
Trimble, Chris, 74
two-way learning, 7–8

uncertainty, 10–11
Unilever, 37, 110
unions, negotiating with, 29–30
universal identity (UID) project,
        154–155
U.S. Defense Department, 66
UTV, 164–166

value chain, 123
value creation, 34–35

Wahhab, Iqbal, 49–50, 51
Walmart, 107
Wang, Haiyan, 109, 112
Welch, Jack, 4, 52, 59–60, 108
Western economies, jugaad
        innovation in, 90–91
World 3.0 (Ghemawat), 98–101
The World Is Flat (Friedman), 98
World One building, 13

About
the Authors

Stuart Crainer and Des Dearlove create and champion business ideas. Stuart and Des are the creators of the Thinkers50 (www.thinkers50.com), the original global ranking of business thought leaders. Their work in this area led *Management Today* to describe them as "market makers par excellence."

Stuart and Des are former columnists at *The (London) Times*, contributing editors to the American magazine *Strategy+Business*, and editors of the bestselling *Financial Times Handbook of Management*. Their books include *The Management Century*, *Gravy Training*, *The Future of Leadership*, and *Generation Entrepreneur*. These books are available in more than 20 languages.

Stuart is the editor of the award-winning *Business Strategy Review*. *Personnel Today* has selected him as one of the most influential people in British people management. Des is an associate fellow of the Saïd Business School at Oxford University and is the author of a bestselling study of the leadership style of Richard Branson. Stuart and Des are adjunct professors at IE Business School.

About The Thinkers50

The Thinkers50 is the definitive global ranking of management thinkers. Its mission is to scan, rank, and share the best business thinking. First published in 2001, the Thinkers50 has been published every two years since then. The ranking was topped in 2011 and 2013 by Harvard Business School's Professor Clayton Christensen. The previous winners were C. K. Prahalad (2009 and 2007), Michael Porter (2005), and Peter Drucker (2003 and 2001).

The ranking is based on voting at the Thinkers50 website and input from a team of advisors led by Stuart Crainer and Des Dearlove. The Thinkers50 has 10 established criteria by which thinkers are evaluated:

- Originality of ideas
- Practicality of ideas
- Presentation style
- Written communication
- Loyalty of followers
- Business sense
- International outlook
- Rigor of research
- Impact of ideas
- Power to inspire